Path of the Seeker

Book Two

More works by the same author:

Path of the Seeker Book One:
The Way of Return
At the Gate of Discipleship
Between the Desert and the Sown
by Nargis Jessie Dowland

Caravan of Souls:
An Introduction to the Sufi Path of Hazrat Inayat Khan
Compiled and edited by Pir Zia Inayat-Khan

*For a complete listing of Sulūk Press
Omega Publications titles see
www.omegapub.com*

Path of the Seeker

Book Two

The Lifted Veil
Wine From the Tavern
The Notebook

by

Nargis Jessie Dowland

With a Biographical Portrait of the Author
by Nancy Barta-Norton

Sulūk Press
New Lebanon New York

Published by Sulūk Press
an imprint of Omega Publications, Inc.
New Lebanon NY
www.omegapub.com

Cover image courtesy of Shutterstock.com
Cover design by Sandra Lillydahl

This edition is printed on acid-free paper
that meets ANSI standard X39–48.

Nargis Jessie Dowland (1866–1953)
Path of the Seeker: Book Two
The Lifted Veil, Wine From the Tavern,
The Notebook

Includes foreword, acknowledgments,
author biography by Nancy Barta-Norton, index
1.Sufism 2. Mysticism 3. Spirituality
I Dowland, Nargis Jessie II. Title

Library of Congress Control Number: 2015960909

Printed and bound in the United States of America
ISBN 978–1–941810–15–6

Contents

Nargis Jessie Dowland
1866–1953

Foreword

THE works of Nargis Jesse Dowland have long been out of print, with only a few copies preserved in public and private collections. A new generation of readers is now invited to read and be inspired by these classics of spirituality, and to follow the author on a journey progressing through the stages of seeking, discovering guidance, and continuing on the pilgrimage toward the ultimate goal of unity with the source of all life.

Path of the Seeker: Book Two, combines two works by Nargis Dowland, *The Lifted Veil*, and *Wine From the Tavern,* with Nargis' personal *Notebook* and a detailed biographical portrait of the author provided by Nancy Barta-Norton. Continuing the journey begun in *Path of the Seeker: Book One*, in this volume the traveler progresses through realms of spiritual experience, encountering the joy of new discoveries on the path of return to the Beloved, while still fulfilling life's duties.

Nargis Dowland was an early editor and publisher of the words of her Sufi teacher, Hazrat Inayat Khan. She used phrases from his writings and those of other spiritual teachers as seed thoughts as the inspirational starting points to inspire her own work.

In keeping with the conventions of her time, Nargis Dowland used masculine pronouns for indeterminate gender and for God. Because this practice is today considered to be biased, every effort has been made to neutralize gender throughout this volume, with the goal of making *Path of the Seeker* more accessible to a contemporary readership. Exception has been made for quoted passages and for poetry in order to preserve the accuracy of the quotes and poetic cadence. Other exceptions include instances where the word "man" is referenced in relation to other related terms such as "hu-man" and "manas" (mind). References to God as Father involve a particular familial concept of the author and were also preserved as originally written. The term "Christ" is sometimes used to refer to the historical Jesus, and at other times appears in a more universal perspective as referring to the Spirit of Guidance. Because of the fluidity and uncertainty of the author's intention regarding these different identifications, the masculine gender of Christ is also preserved.

Acknowledgments

Path of the Seeker is the result of the persistent and dedicated efforts of Nancy Barta-Norton, who used her professional librarian skills to locate and obtain copies of the writings of Nargis Dowland and her correspondence with Hazrat Inayat Khan. Nancy also provided the author's biography found in *Path of the Seeker: Book Two*, which is based on the results of her extensive, in-depth research on the life and work of Nargis Dowland. Without Nancy's devoted work, *Path of the Seeker* would not have been brought into existence.

Many thanks are also due to those who have with kindness and generosity provided the materials, permissions, and advice that have made it possible to make Nargis Dowland and her works known once again to today's readers.

Qahira Wirgman and the Nekbkaht Foundation in Suresnes, France, have provided invaluable assistance with advice, photographs, copies of Nargis Dowland's writings and personal documents. Murshid Ameen Carp and Murshid Karimbaksh Witteveen generously gave the International Sufi Movement's permission to publish *At the Gate of Discipleship*, *Between the Desert and the Sown*, and *The Lifted Veil*. Hamida Verlinden from the International Sufi Headquarters in The Hague, The Netherlands, provided copies of correspondence between Nargis Dowland and her teacher, Hazrat Inayat Khan. And invaluable editorial advice and assistance was provided by Cannon Labrie.

The Lifted Veil

Shall any gazer see with mortal eyes,
Or any searcher know by mortal mind;
Veil after veil will lift—but there must be
Veil upon veil behind.

—Edwin Arnold
The Light of Asia

1

TURN, O pilgrim of the mystic path, turn from self to God.

Through the unreal, seek the real; through the shadows, realize the light. From the clouds of illusion that cover you, lift your eyes, that the sacred sun may illumine your way.

Gradually indraw your consciousness from all the bodies of the soul, until the heart is reached and the hidden self uncovered, which is the journey's end; for to live internally with God is the goal of the mystic.

Then will the heaven and the earth lie at your feet, for, verily, you are greater than they.

2

THE mystic teaching that the whole earthly life is illusion is very difficult to realize, but when the first veil is lifted one can see and understand that this is so because of the ever-changingness of all material life; and one knows that all things that change must one day cease to be.

When travelers upon the spiritual path have made this knowledge a reality, they begin to search for the unchanging, and never cease their seeking until they have found God, Who alone is everlasting.

The One Light in a world of shadows, the One Reality in the midst of illusion.

3

Dost thou know why so many obstacles have been set up on the path? It is in order that the devotee may gradually develop strength to be able to see the Beloved without a veil.[1]

—Sharaf al-Din Maneri

IT is the universal experience of all true seekers of God that after the first wonder and rapture of spiritual vision, which, as it were, intoxicates the soul whose eyes are opening, there follows a period of darkness, depression, and doubt, far worse than anything they had known before their feet were set upon the path. This is natural, for spiritual awakening rouses a soul from a state of sleep to keen perception; and unless at this stage disciples are able to keep in their hearts the remembrance that light is the one reality and darkness the great illusion, they may be overwhelmed by the shadows. A great faith, a great courage, and infinite patience are needed to convey the traveler safely through this necessary stage upon the path to God. The teaching given by all masters of divine wisdom is that light must be sought through darkness, and reality through unreality; but the inner meaning of this is seldom understood. The most usual interpretation is that spiritual progress is made from darkness to light, and from the unreal to the real, which in some sense, of course, is true, but refers to the final stage of liberation where thought cannot follow. It is not by turning away from the unreal before it is understood that reality can be found, but by going

1 Sharaf al-Din Maneri, *Letters From a Sufi Teacher*, trans. Baijnath Singh (London: Theosophical Publishing Society, 1909).

through it, which is a contrary process and cannot be realized until disciples can make it part of the their own being. This realization is totally different from an intellectual conception, and means rising above illusion and thus controlling it. When this can be accomplished, unreality has no more power to hold them.

Such an experience cannot be expressed in words. Suggestions only may be offered to one who is possibly feeling bewildered by finding darkness where one expected light. In a world ruled by duality, or the pairs of opposites, the inner truth of all things must be gained by knowledge of their opposites; for only by comparison is it possible to judge. Therefore, whosoever has been granted a vision of divine beauty and from before whose eyes the first veil has been lifted, sooner or later is brought face-to-face with illusion in order that they may test the truth of their own spiritual sight, which cannot be fully awakened until after such testing. Again and again, the false will be mistaken for the true, and the true for the false; for each plays many parts in life's drama, with truth sometimes hiding under the garment of falsehood, and untruth assuming the robe of truth. The disciple must learn to recognize both under all conditions, independent of the outer garment; for unless unreality is seen and recognized in all its many phases and impersonations, reality, of which illusion is the shadow, can never be reached. "This divine illusion of Mine caused by the qualities is hard to pierce; they who come to Me, they cross over this illusion."[2] The greatest illusion of all is met when the disciples are face-to-face with the embodiment of their own thoughts and desires, and the test of their spiritual sight is that they may recognize it as such.

But let not the aspirants be discouraged by any difficulties they may have to meet upon this path; for, although appar-

2 *Bhagavad Gita: The Lord's Song*, trans Annie Besant (London: Theosophical Publishing Society, 1896).

ently each test must be passed through alone, in reality there is unseen guidance at every step of the way. "He who seeth Me everywhere, and seeth everything in Me, of him will I never lose hold, and he shall never lose hold of Me."[3] Also let the aspirant remember that it is in response to the demand made by one's own soul that the opportunity is given to pass through darkness to seek light; none other can compel or even invite.

It is the hero souls, demanding light at any cost, even though they walk through hell itself to seek it, who pass this way; and that same quality and power in the human soul that makes such a demand will also supply courage and strength with which to face all difficulties.

Therefore let the disciple be of good cheer, and fear not, for "He that overcometh shall inherit all things; and I will be his God, and he shall be My son."[4]

3 Ibid.

4 Revelations 21:7.

4

FEAR not, O pilgrim upon the path to God; fear not to empty your heart of aught save God; heed not the words of those who would tell you that this is a hard and lonely path to travel, and will shut you away from sympathy with your fellow humans; hat to seek your own salvation is a selfish action; rather should you go down among, and work and suffer with those in the underworld of sin, to seek and save them. This is a subtle temptation that all those who are seeking God will encounter at some period of their journey. "The stage of acceptance with the people is the slipping-place of the saints." And until the spiritual eyes of the disciple are opened, it will be very difficult to see with clear vision; for those who are unselfishly working in the slums of great cities seemingly achieve great deeds. It is true that the men and women doing such work are noble of soul; it is also true that such work is needed, and "Inasmuch as ye have done it unto one of the least of these, my brethren, ye have done it unto me."[1]

But in the life of the disciple there is another stage before final liberation, and to reach this it is necessary that the heart should be still and empty; so still that it could not vibrate to anything that earth might offer, and empty of all belonging to the personal life, even to be known among people as a reliever of pain and suffering. "God is veiled from the heart of the man who sees his proper actions."[2] The souls reaching this stage upon the return journey could never be deaf to the

1 Matthew 25:40.

2 Fani, Muhammed Muhsin, *The Dabistan, or School of Manners*, trans. by David Shea and Anthony Troyer (London: Allen and Co. 1843). 18.

cries of humanity or dead to their sorrows; but they give help in a different way and seldom through their own personalities, so that those receiving their help and consolation do not know from whence it comes. They are called *the blessed ones*, the ministers of God who do God's pleasure; for in this material world God uses the still and empty hearts of men and women through which to pour God's consolation, healing sympathy, and understanding love upon God's suffering children.

Someone in their own personality can give but feeble help and love to the sleeping soul. Not until a person has lost all consciousness of self can one be used to reflect God upon any other human soul; but the heart of such a one can never feel empty or alone. Rather is it filled with joy inexpressible; for the experience of being used as an instrument of God, to focus healing and consolation upon the sick and sorrowful, that God's love and light may reach those in need, brings a happiness beyond all telling, and which no one takes away.[3]

3 "And your joy no man taketh from you." John 16:22.

5

Then opened he their understanding, that they might understand the scriptures.

—Luke 24:45

THE spiritual world cannot be perceived unless the inner senses, which belong to the spirit, are active within, as the physical world cannot be contacted if the physical senses are inactive. It is for this reason that those who aspire to tread the path of return should seek the guidance of a spiritual teacher, as there is a danger in making active the inner centers without the guidance and help of one who understands by personal experience, just as there is danger in making chemical experiments without the instruction of an experienced teacher.

A teacher upon the path should not be sought in order that the teacher may impart knowledge and wisdom to the seeker, although to some extent one may do so, but for the real help the teacher is able to give in showing aspirants how to develop their own spiritual body so that all the centers belonging to that body shall become active, enabling the seekers to see for themselves the answer to every problem life brings them.

This is the only way that spiritual knowledge can ever be known, for there are no words in the human physical brain by which one can convey to another the things of the spirit.

The opening of these inner centers should never be attempted alone or by instruction found in books, for it enables aspirants to respond to every kind of vibration. Their spiritual sight and hearing becoming keen, they see and feel hurtful and terrible sights and sounds, as well as beautiful and harmonious ones. This is a truth that the ignorant cannot understand; confusing spirit with goodness, they think that one who has attained spiritual vision can only contact those things which are beautiful and virtuous. But the real meaning of spirit is essence, and a person whose spiritual eyes are opened can see the essence of all things. Whatever the glance falls upon this person, will see its inner essence, whether it be good or whether it be evil. Therefore, if one enters into the world of spirit unprepared for such sights and sounds, and unaware of their real meaning, the rhythm of one's life may be broken and the mind unbalanced.

A disciple who has the guidance of a real teacher need have no fear of this danger if the disciple faithfully carries out the instructions received. But it is very important that there should be no shadow of doubt of the guide; for directly there is any mistrust in the mind of one whose inner senses are opening—and consequently extremely sensitive—the entrance of astral entities is made possible, and these will obsess the mind with every kind of undesirable thought; for when doubt opens the door the devil can walk in.

It is for this reason essential that no one should seek spiritual guidance from anyone in whom one cannot place implicit trust; for at almost every step of the way, the faith and trust of the disciple is tested by every kind of suggestion, both from within and from without.

This testing is an absolute necessity for the safety of the disciples, for no spiritual teacher would dare to fully open the sacred centers of aspirants unless, by such testing, the teacher had made quite sure that they could be safely trusted to keep each one's own note in tune amid the thousands of conflicting vibrations that fill the earth and that, by reason of the awakened senses, they would be conscious of. But if the heart of such a one is ever resting in the thought of God, that disciple may walk in sure and certain faith that one will reach the goal of one's desire.

6

Let not him that seeketh cease from his search until he find; and when he finds he shall wonder; wondering he shall reach the Kingdom, and when he reaches the Kingdom he shall have rest.[1]

—*Sayings of Jesus*

HUMAN beings can never find God unless they seek for God, although in reality God is nearer to them than the ocean to the fishes. But it is only during the times of seeking that the eyes of the soul are open to behold God. The search itself opens them; at all other times they are closed. For this reason the seeking must be undertaken by each one individually, and no one can give to another the vision of God.

God, the all-loving Father, hides the Divine Self that each may receive soul-sight by their seeking, although all the time God is so close that all things whatsoever one thinks in one's heart are known unto God. But in order that the human soul shall fulfill the purpose for which it came to earth, experience all things, subdue all things, and return with the open vision, or soul-vision, God plays with us an eternal game of hide-and-seek to lure us ever onward in our search, and so prevent the deadly lethargy that enwraps the soul whose eyes remain closed.

1 Marshall, Troward, "The Rebirth of Wonder." *Christian Register,* August 10, 1911. 848.

7

Kabir says, "As you may never find the forest if you ignore the tree, so He may never be found in abstractions."[1]

—*Kabir*

IT is impossible for the human mind to formulate any idea of the Absolute. Spirit can only be perceived by spirit, but the need for worship is an innate need of every human soul; and people must find some means by which they may express that which is latent within them. "Each pilgrim has his own stage according to his aspiration."[2] Therefore, when a person becomes conscious of this need, the creative mind evolves a God whom one can worship, for "The God Who is intelligible to man is made by man himself; but what is beyond his intelligence is the reality."[3]

The instinctive desire to worship is the call of the Beloved to the lover. The act of worship is the answer, from the deeps of one's being, of the lover to the Beloved. It has been said that one may be known by the size of one's God, for according to a person's nature, is the God Whom one worships. "The faith of each is shaped to his own nature, O Bharata."[4]

As a person grows in wisdom and the knowledge of spiritual truth, which is a gradual unfoldment from within, so will the size of that person's God increase until the realization comes that all is God, and that the whole universe with its myriad lives exists in God as an infinitesimal part of the One Life.

1 Kabir, *One Hundred Poems of Kabir*, trans. Rabindranath Tagore. (London: Macmillan, 1915).

2 Sharaf al-Din Maneri, *Letters From a Sufi Teacher*.

3 Inayat Khan, Hazrat. *The Gayan*.

4 Bhagavad Gita.

Thus to the God-realized, all things and beings become objects of worship, for in everything one sees God reflected.

But such a one would never, even in thought, belittle the object of another's veneration; for this person would understand that as worship is a necessity for spiritual growth, so, until people can perceive the whole, they must worship in part.

> *For we know in part and we prophesy in part; but when that which is perfect is come, then that which is in part shall be done away.*
>
> *—II Corinthians 13:9-10*

8

Seek Him that maketh the seven stars and Orion, and turneth the shadow of death into the morning, and maketh the day dark with night; that calleth for the waters of the sea and poureth them out upon the face of the earth. The Lord is his name.

—Amos 5:8

If thou seek Him, He will be found of thee.

–1 Chronicles 28:9

IT is the lure of the unknown that draws human beings upward, enabling them to stand upright, ready to face and overcome all difficulties. That which is known has no mystery of attraction. People may worship the known, but they will remain upon their knees. Inherent in everyone is the love of adventure, of seeking and finding for oneself. This shows even in little children who love to play games of hiding and seeking; in those who travel thousands of miles, unheeding cost or discomfort, to add a rare treasure to their store; and in the brave souls who risk all, even life itself, to discover something hitherto unknown to humanity. It would not satisfy any of these to have their objective found for them, for the joy of adventure lies in the search itself. A moment of ecstasy is experienced when any discovery is made, even by a child who, unaided, finds a common wildflower.

It is, therefore, that God has used every living and breathing thing in the universe under which to hide the glory of God's presence, that people may have the supreme ecstasy of daily and hourly making a fresh discovery. There is no joy greater or more uplifting than the joy of adventure in the spiritual life, and will this take one through many dangerous places, almost unconscious of the difficulties, so intent is one upon the great treasure hunt for God.

It is said by the mystic that God has veiled the Divine Self with seventy thousand veils in order that a seeker may experience seventy thousand joys; and when one has found and lifted any of the veils that hide the living God, the lips are sealed by the unveiling. To none other can this discovery be made known, lest from the other, one joy of discovery be taken away.

The spirit of joy greets the true seeker of God when one realizes that, by lifting any one of the veils that cover all things and beings, one has proof of the presence of God; and once having realized this, nothing could keep one from continuing the search. Thus, absorbed in the seeking, the seeker goes ever onward, following the divine trail until past and future hold no meaning; for the present so full, so intoxicatingly full of wonder, obliterates past pain and future fear.

There are naturally many dangers for aspirants upon the path of seeking, and they must have the guidance of one who knows the way in order to travel in safety. For ere they set foot upon this path, they must have faithfully fulfilled their life's duties. Not one can remain undischarged that, if so left, would have power to cause them to look back; for if at this stage they were to do so, the rhythm of their seeking would break. Only a master of the path is able to give the necessary instructions for taking this journey. If the aspirants have not found a teacher it is because they are not quite ready; and if they will faithfully search their hearts they will find the cause of their unreadiness. "When the cry of the disciple has reached a certain pitch, the teacher comes to answer it."[1]

It is quite impossible that one who utters that cry will ever be overlooked, but the wine of Christ can only be given to

1 Inayat Khan, *The Gayan.*

those who have been prepared to receive it. For in that divine intoxication, the self of the seeker is lost in the Beloved.

9

THOSE who seek for signs and wonders need not look for them in the séance room or in messages from the other side given through mediums, clairvoyants, or automatic writing. If a person had knowledge of one atom of matter, a thousand mysteries would unfold before that person's view, although a thousand years of study would not suffice to reveal its marvels. Ordinary human life is full of wonders, and the greatest miracle ever performed can be seen and understood by one whose eyes are open to behold the daily and hourly happenings in what on earth is called *nature*, but which, really speaking, is an activity of God. These are so wonderful that human imagination fails to grasp their significance; and yet, in one's inner life, one has the capacity of comprehension.

Not all the books ever written, not all the knowledge orally imparted can give the wisdom revealed through concentration and meditation upon the secrets of nature.

The history of so small a thing as a flower seed could not be contained in a library of books. But to the people of God the book of nature is open; and even a grain of corn speaks to them and will reveal its past, present, and future. Its present is the result of a past flowering, part of whose fruitage was made into sustenance that nourished and became one with many beings of a higher evolution; absorbed by them until what was necessary for their growth had been abstracted and then given out again through various ways, in countless atoms of physical matter; to pass and repass through millions of other beings in one unending, ever-moving lifestream, forming part of numberless forms. All this, including the shape, color, and characteristics of the plant from which it drew its life and of which it retains the inherent capacity of becoming a beginningless past and an endless future hidden in an eternal present, is represented to the eye of a seer by a single minute and, to the outer eye, quite insignificant grain of corn.

A blade of grass would reveal its mysteries, its message of the oneness of life. Common field grass, over which people walk unheeding and unconscious that it is part of God's life, nourishes and becomes one with the cattle who eat it, and who pass on the life in their own bodies to sustain and nourish human beings.

Nothing is lost, nothing dies, nothing is useless; but everything is changed, molded, and remolded. Form after form created, form after form destroyed, until God's plan for the evolution of a universe is perfected and complete.

This is the real sacrament, and to each object and being is said, "Take, eat; this is my body."[1]

1 Mark 14:22.

10

IT is sometimes a cause of bewilderment to many who profess to be seeking God that they should make so little progress upon the path. There are several reasons why this should be so. In the first place, to the real seeker there could never be any sense of progress, for one whose eyes are fixed upon the goal could not be conscious of one's own development—but of true seekers there are few. The majority are seeking God with one eye, and their own advancement with the other. And until the vision be made one, the goal of the seeker cannot be reached, for no one can walk in two ways at the same time.

There is an Eastern saying: "A true guru will give to all who ask of him that thing which each man most desires, whether it be good or whether it be evil." This is difficult of comprehension unless it is clearly understood that one can only receive those things, the seeds of which are already within one's own heart.

Whatever reaches fulfillment in human life does so by reason of the awakening to life of that which is latent within, which, unless awakened by desire, will never reach fruition. In every person are the positive nuclei of good and evil. And according to the rhythm of one's life, will the vibratory action of these nuclei, when made active or awake, draw upon them their necessary complementary negative particles. This results in activity, or the creation of the desired form. Therefore, for those who voluntarily seek a spiritual teacher with the desire that they may be awakened from the sleep of illusion, the action of the teacher's presence upon them is as that of the sun upon the earth, which brings to birth all the hidden seeds, be they flowers or weeds. "To every seed its own body,"[1] whether it be a rose or whether it be a thistle. The seeds that are gathered for future sowing must depend upon each person's own desire. If this greatest longing is for the expansion of self, and the seeds of greatness are within a person, that person will become great for a season. If power is the desire of the heart, and is latent within, one will obtain power to carry out all that one wishes; but in so doing there is grave danger that one may oneself be destroyed by the power thus created. If, however, the sight be single, and the greatest desire, beside which every other thing fades into nothingness, is to find God, the seeker will surely find God.

The path a seeker travels rests with the seeker's own self. The teacher can impart the impetus but cannot choose the path of a disciple, neither can the teacher tread it for the disciple. But the teacher can, and does, give directions that, if faithfully followed, will enable each one to eradicate all harmful desires from the heart. Blessed are those whose desire is toward God; verily, they shall inherit a kingdom.

1 1 Corinthians 15:38.

11

THOSE who aspire to tread the spiritual path are oftentimes bewildered when they see one whom they know to be a great soul, or a messenger of God, suffering the ordinary ills of humanity. They think that these great ones should be above all physical pain or discomfort; and when they find that this is not so, will say among themselves, "This one, whom we thought great, cannot be a master, or surely he could not be as mortal man, subject to fatigue or illness. A real master would be above such things."

It is the same in all ages. Those around Jesus during his earthly life thought just the same. "He saves others, himself he cannot save. If he can, then we will believe that he is the Son of God."[1] They demanded, as many today demand, that a messenger of God should conform to their ideas of what the messenger should be, or the messenger is not from God.

A daily and hourly crucifixion is the life of the messenger who comes in a physical body to a world of scoffers and unbelievers, bringing life to those who are dead in sin. How can they, even the few who would tread the spiritual path, understand the laws governing the holy ones who, when working in the material world, voluntarily limit themselves to its conditions in order that none of the ills to which humankind is subject may be unknown to them?

The way of God is as different from humanity's way as is light from darkness. "'For My thoughts are not your thoughts, neither are your ways My ways,' saith the Lord."[2]

1 Matthew 27:42.

2 Isaiah 55:8.

Very few would-be disciples are willing to "become as little children,"[3] receiving instructions in faith and trust. It is difficult for one who has traveled far and gathered stores of intellectual knowledge to bring to a spiritual teacher a mind emptied of facts, or to refrain from measuring the teaching received by one's own small measure of understanding. One is slow to realize that "The false ego is a false god; when the false god is destroyed, the true God arrives."[4] This is the lesson that all candidates on the path must learn; and how can those, whose feet have not yet taken even the first step, judge the actions of one who has trodden it? They have not begun to understand the meaning of the sacred prayer, uttered by all the great souls who have attained sonship: "Not my will, but Thine, be done."[5] To utter these words in deed and in truth is the last and supreme sacrifice. It means the surrender to the Father of a perfected personality. As Browning expresses it: "The submission of man's nothing-perfect to God's All-Complete; as by each new obeisance in spirit, I climb to His feet!."[6]

In this sacramental act of submission, all powers gained that could be used for the help or glorification of the personal self are transmuted into a never-failing power to help suffering humanity; and from henceforth only the will of God works through those who, having completely surrendered their personal will, are called *masters of compassion*. And in them, whatever the Father wills, although often incomprehensible to humanity, is done. "How unsearchable are the His judgments, and His ways past finding out! For who hath known the mind of the Lord?"[7]

---

3 Matthew 18:3.

4 Inayat Khan, *The Gayan.*

5 Luke 22:42.

6 Browning, Robert, "Saul."

7 Romans 11:33–34.

12

O taste and see that the Lord is good: blessed is the man that trusteth in Him."

—Psalm 34:8

THESE words are, as are all inspired utterances, capable of many interpretations, for they contain a profound truth applicable to all religions in every age, which is perceived and interpreted according to the power of insight of the interpreter.

In the words, "O, taste and see that the Lord is good," the seer can perceive the solution of the whole mystery of God-realization. All the bodies that humans use for their expression must be sustained by suitable nourishment, otherwise they are not complete human beings. For if any one of these bodies is starved, humans are unable to express themselves upon the plane of being to which that body belongs. It is therefore necessary for human perfecting that a person shall receive physical, emotional, mental, and spiritual sustenance.

For the physical body, physical food is needed. The mental body must be sustained by thought; the body of emotions requires love for its growth; but the spiritual body can only be fed by God-realization. In every case the food must be not only eaten but digested, for it must become part of the body it feeds. In other words, the body becomes that of which it partakes, which, when digested, ceases to be a something separate and apart. The grace said before food by a religious sect in India, "I, God, eat Thee, God," is an acknowledgment of this paradox.

The methods of the scientist to discover the secret of life and those of the mystic are equally ways to God; because, ultimately, all paths end in God. But the difference between knowledge of God and realization is great and difficult to explain in words. The following allegory may help to unfold the idea.

A scientist and a mystic traveled to a country in which there grew a famous fruit tree, said to contain the elements of life, in order that they might know and understand the nature and growth of the tree and test the properties of its fruit.

The scientist made careful and minute calculation; tested and measured the tree; opened, examined, and analyzed the fruit, tabulating and weighing the elements of which it was composed. The mystic did none of these things. The mystic simply ate the fruit. The result was that the scientist knew all there was to know; but the mystic was fed and refreshed, because, believing the fruit to be life-giving, the mystic tasted it.

Jesus said to his disciples: "As the living Father hath sent me, and I live by the Father, so he that eateth me, even he shall live by me."[1]

Whosoever can unfold the mystery hidden in this teaching, to them will be given the secret of realization.

To realize a truth one must absorb it into oneself. There is no other way. So long as one stands apart to analyze it, one can never feel its life-giving properties. Nevertheless the person who is able to know and also to realize, is the master of life; for "He makes the law his upper garment, and the mystic path his inner garment."[2]

> *Hereby know we that we dwell in Him, and He in us,*
> *because He hath given us of His Spirit.*
>
> —*1 John 4:13*

1 John 6:57.

2 Mahmud ibn 'Abd al-Karim Shabistari, *The Mystic Rose Garden,* trans. Edward Whinfield (London: Trubner and Company, 1880).

13

Disciples may be likened to the strings of the soul-echoing vina; mankind unto its sounding-board; the hand that sweeps it to the tuneful breath of the great World Soul. The string that fails to answer 'neath the Master's touch in dulcet harmony with all the others, breaks —and is cast away.[1]

—*H.P. Blavatsky*

IT is the work of the great ones, who from the inner worlds bring to earth a message destined to help humanity, to fashion the suitable form to hold a living truth.

This form must be gradually built from the human material available until an organism is evolved, which can then be used as a channel for spreading the message of God in the material world.

As the organism must necessarily be composed of human beings, more or less unfitted to be so used, the task is oftentimes long and difficult; and is in some measure made more so when the individuals forming the channel have a misconception of the plan and of their own importance with regard to it. By thinking of themselves as separate channels of divine force, set apart and used by the master for the master's work, they fail to realize that the organism as a whole (of which they are but an infinitesimal part) is the real channel. They also forget that, unless one can merge one's own personality in the good of the whole, one cannot remain even a part; for all must work in harmony by taking the place allotted to them and faithfully fulfilling their own particular task.

1 Blavatsky, Helena Petrovna, *The Voice of Silence* ((London: Theosophical Publishing Society, 1889).

None is greater than another. Each one is needed in their own place; but if everyone wishes to take another's place, there is naturally discord and confusion as there would be disharmony in an orchestra if, for instance, a violinist tried to play the music written for the harp; if a pianist ceased playing because the pianist considered the part unimportant; or a drummer failed to beat the drum at the right moment because the drummer was arguing about the method. For a symphony to be correctly played, each player must be intent upon their own part and play in rhythm with the conductor. Those unwilling to cooperate could not remain members of an orchestra.

Of course, it is a fact that individuals are sometimes used as separate channels; but when this is so, they themselves, in their physical consciousness, are entirely unconscious of being so used unless they have reached the stage in evolution where such knowledge can be safely held. This is, however, a high stage seldom attained by humans. A wise one has said, "And this I know, that when the gods have use for us they blindfold us, because if we should see and comprehend the outcome, we should grow so vain that not even the gods could save us from destruction."[2]

As a rule, no one can be used and be conscious of the using.

If anyone says they are a vessel used by the master, they will never be fit for the master's use. If anyone thinks they are selfless, their hearts are filled with self. They must be that which they desire to be thought—a very different thing, and a process of spiritual growth.

Only through empty hearts from which self has been entirely eliminated can the Master Musician send forth the note of unity, which will unite all the dwellers upon earth into one harmonious whole.

---

2 Mundy, Talbot, *OM; the Secret of Ahbor Valley* (Indianapolis: Bobbs-Merrill, 1924).

14

Our celestial spirit is free to eternity, tho' for a short while we have the shape and figure of a man.[1]

—*Jalal ad-Din Rumi*

THE inner teaching of Sufism is for the purpose of unveiling the mystery of God-identification, which is the process of the second birth. "The first birth is the birth of man, the second birth is the birth of God."[2]

God is immortal, humanity partakes of mortality. A human, as a created being, has a beginning and, therefore, must also have an end. Every created thing contains within itself the limit of the span of its created life; and when the hour strikes, the creation disintegrates or, as it is called, is destroyed.

A human being—a stage in the soul's life—is a thought, held for a time and then is no more.

The human soul, in order to become immortal, must be born again, for "That which is born of the flesh is flesh; and that which is born of the spirit is spirit";[3] and "Whatsoever is born of God overcometh the world."[4]

While the soul, as a human being, identifies itself with mind, it cannot attain immortality because its desire is individual expression in physical life as a separated being, which necessarily must come to an end. "Who lives with his individual

1 Jalal ad-Din Rumi, *Selected Poems from the Divani Shamsi Tabriz*, trans. Reynolds Nicholson. (Cambridge: Cambridge University Press, 1952). 215.

2 Inayat Khan, *The Gayan*.

3 John 3:6.

4 1 John 5:4.

self will live as long as his individual self lives, here and hereafter. And who lives with God will live the everlasting life of God."[5]

Eternal life is the soul's birthright, but must be claimed through the experience of a new birth and the realization of its true origin. "Marvel not that I said unto thee, ye must be born again."[6] "Except a man be born again, he cannot see the kingdom of God."[7]

Human birth on the physical plane means an initiation into conditions totally different from those of prenatal life, to which one must gradually become accustomed. The same law operates at the second birth: it is an initiation of a human soul into unfamiliar conditions. The whole outlook is altered and, as a little child, a person must learn to walk upon the spiritual path. One begins stumblingly and hesitatingly at first, but in the end surely and steadily maintaining one's balance, until, at the soul's coming of age, the seeker is no more a child but the acknowledged son of the Father.

> *The Spirit itself beareth witness with our spirit, that we are the children of God; and if children, then heirs.*
>
> *—Romans 8:16–17*

5 Inayat Khan, "The Destiny of the Soul."

6 John 3:7.

7 John 3:3.

15

O, TRAVELER upon the path to God, rest not content in your prayers and fastings, for they, of themselves, will never take you into God's presence.

So long as humans are humans, there must be a continual striving between their higher and lower nature, the true and the false ego; for the power of mastering difficulties by rising above them is the privilege given to humanity, who by this means becomes *hu-man*.[1] But if, for one moment, one loses one's own center of balance, a person cannot stand as a human should stand: upright, with head turned Godward and feet upon earth, the ruler of one's own domain.

If you are treading the balanced path, and can keep the center steady, then as you aspire and go forward, so will the power and activity increase on both sides.

The secret of balance lies in keeping the eyes of the soul fixed upon God, while the feet are firmly planted upon earth. A person who is able to accomplish this cannot fail to remain steadfast; for by contemplation upon the love of God and the beauty of God's perfection, the human soul, which, however deeply encased in matter, is ever seeking union with the divine, will be drawn upwards to God as the magnetized needle imprisoned in a compass is inevitably drawn towards the mystic north. "Only thyself veils thy Self." By meditation upon this teaching the disciple may understand the mystery of divine alchemy that transmutes the self into the Self, where one is lost in God.

1 The word *Hu* is one of the most ancient names for the Divine Being.

16

The jewel is lost in the mud, and all are seeking for it;
Some look for it in the east, and some in the west;
Some in the water and some amongst stones.
But the servant Kabir has appraised it at its true value,
and has wrapped it with care in the end of the mantle of his heart.[1]

—*Kabir*

ALTHOUGH all things are open to human sight, one can only see that for which one is seeking. "But if our *gospel* be hid, it is hid to them that are lost, in whom the god of this world hath blinded the minds of them which believe not."[2]

In every age there live those who resent the fact that the wisdom teaching, or the mysteries, should be (as they believe) withheld from the people and reserved for the few, which results in the formation of numberless groups and societies of people who claim to be able to interpret what they call *occult* or *esoteric truths*. These people are quite prepared to explain to all the ways of God and the mystery of existence. Verily, they are as the blind leading the blind, for they are ignorant of the fact that no one can understand the mysteries until their own spiritual perceptions are open to recognize that for which they are seeking, and to receive understanding of the many veils that cover reality. This same fact is operative in material things, for if those who search for gold and precious stones had no knowledge of the outer appearance

1 Kabir, *Songs of Kabir* trans. Rabindranath Tagore (New York: Macmillan Company, 1915).

2 2 Corinthians 4:3–4.

of what they were seeking, they would fail to recognize them and might even throw away as useless, some priceless jewel.

The reason that the knowers of the mysteries of life do not communicate their knowledge to all is not because they are unwilling to do so, but because they cannot talk to those who are unable to understand the language in which they speak. And although they are always ready to show an earnest and sincere seeker of divine wisdom how this may be learned, it is only the aspirant with singleness of purpose, to whom the search is the one thing in life that matters, who will have the necessary patience; for although in reality it is a language of perfect simplicity, in practice it is full of paradox.

No one need be afraid of not being able to find a teacher if they are ready to receive instruction. Those who have not found are not yet ready to receive. When they are, they will seek their guru, and never cease from their seeking until they find.

There are always some of the great ones in the world waiting to impart their knowledge to anyone who is willing to be taught; but they must be sought. And the difficulty with most people is that, although they want to be told the answer to their questioning, they are impatient at having to learn the only language by which it can be imparted.

That which prevents anyone from partaking of the mysteries of God is a person's own inability to perceive them; for nothing can be withheld from one who has eyes to see; and no power in heaven or earth could close them, save only the shadow of the false ego causing darkness where there should be light.

While people stand with their backs to God, they can see nothing but the shadow of themselves. To see the light by which all things are illuminated, they must turn round and face the light, which is God. For in that vision the consciousness of the small self will fade away as before the rising sun.

"For there is nothing covered that shall not be revealed"[3] to one who has turned from darkness to light.

> *For within Thee is the fountain of life: and in Thy light shall we see light.*
>
> *—Psalm 36:9*

3 Luke 12:2.

17

GOD is love, and it is only by developing to its utmost capacity the power of loving, without thought of gain for self or of return for love given, that any human soul is enabled to understand and respond to the love of God.

Most people expect to be loved in return for love, and when they help the needy, expect them to be grateful for such help. There is nothing wrong in this attitude for those who feel thus, but for a disciple on the path to God something more is needed. For a disciple, the only return for love given should be the privilege of loving; and the only gratitude for help rendered, the satisfaction of having helped. And when this stage is reached there is a further one still when the disciple unconsciously gives love and help to all, because the disciple's whole horizon is filled with the image of God. Then all things become merged into one glorious vision of the perfection of love, harmony, and beauty, until the disciple sees all living beings as one's own self, an expression of the One Life.

The great need of the soul who is seeking union with God is to develop love for love's sake, and be able, at the same time, to be detached from the object loved—a difficult but necessary achievement for one who is treading this path.

The full realization of love does not come to all. There are few who have courage to face the sunlight of God's presence wherein everything, save the pure gold of love itself, is turned away. The majority live all their lives in its shadow and are content with love's counterfeit. Its inner mysteries are only unfolded to those whom life has called to pass through the gates of sacrifice, for they have been prepared by suffering to receive the ecstasy of joy.

A person who has never touched the depths of love cannot stand upon the heights. But whosoever has experienced, even for one moment, the upliftment of love's sacrifice or tasted but one drop of its sacramental wine, is lifted above its alternating sorrows and joys, its hopes and fears, its pleasures and its pains. For this person has stood in the living presence of God, Who is Love; and that remembrance will remain through the rest of the journey. For "one day is with the Lord as a thousand years."[1]

---

1 2 Peter 3:8.

18

In the beginning was the Word.

—John 1:1

BEFORE anything can materialize in the physical world it must be first given forth: uttered or spoken. By the power of creative thought, mental images of all things come into being but cannot take form or become embodied in the material world until the word of power has been uttered. Sometimes it is necessary for the word to be repeated for many years before the form is complete and ready to hold the living spirit, which, clothed in mental matter and already existing in the world of ideas, is awaiting the time of its manifestation. The actual speaking in words of an idea or mental creation causes a particular note or vibration to sound, which, if the note is in tune with the vibratory chord to which it belongs, will in time, according to the power of its creator, draw around itself the necessary physical atoms to mold the idea into the form or forms needed for its expression. Thus an uttered word can become solid and materialized. Saint John called Jesus Christ *the embodied Word of life.*[1] All forms, whether a building of stone or the human body itself, must be brought to birth from the world of ideas into the world of names and forms by the power of vibration, which alone can build a material body.

By concentration and meditation upon the mystery of the spoken word, the disciple will realize another aspect: that of the power of prayer and its importance in the spiritual life, which the great ones of all religions have taught their disci-

1 See John 1:14.

ples and have themselves practiced; for, as a great mystic has said, "The secret of prayer is inexpressible."

When a word of power is uttered by one who understands the mystery of sound, the act of speaking aloud breaks thought into millions of reproductions of itself, spreading in etheric waves throughout the physical world, influencing thousands of people and producing a harvest of human thought and action; for everyone whose heart is attuned can receive and respond to thought, which is thus broadcast by a master mind. As the flower must yield or utter its seeds for its own reproduction, as the clouds must break to give forth water to nourish the earth, which, in turn again, yields up its moisture, so must prayer be uttered or remain unproductive.

> *For as the rain cometh down, and the snow from heaven, and returneth not thither, but watereth the earth, and maketh it bring forth and bud that it may give seed to the sower, and bread to the eater, so shall my word be that goeth forth out of my mouth: it shall not return unto me void, but it shall accomplish that which I please, and it shall prosper in the thing whereto I sent it.*
>
> —*Isaiah 55:10–11*

19

Keep God in remembrance till self is forgotten.
—Jalal ad-Din Rumi

IT is the nature of the soul to identify itself with what it gazes upon. Therefore, so long as the mind holds self before its view, the soul calls itself *human* and remains in a world of mental images of human creation, which is so full of *I* that there is no room for God. As it is said in the teaching of Shri Krishna, "The mind is the slayer of the real; let the disciple slay the slayer."[1] When the heart can reflect and steadily hold the image of God before the soul, then will it identify itself with God, of Whom it is, from Whom it came, and to Whom it must return. But the return journey cannot begin until the soul wakens from its dream of *I*; for, in this dream of identification with the false ego, it sees itself as a separate being, important to itself and to the world in which it is sojourning, and therefore has no desire to lose its separateness in God. For so long as it wanders in the dream life, feeling sufficient unto itself, the eyes remain closed to reality. To see God, the soul must awaken from dreams of its little self and claim its royal heritage of union with the Divine; for when once the beauty of the Perfect One is realized, *I* is remembered no more. However long and however deep the dream may be, to each soul comes the hour of its awakening, when it arises from the unreal to the real, from human to God.

1 Blavatsky, Helena Petrovna, *The Voice of Silence.*

20

ALL are seeking for joy, either consciously or unconsciously, and each one thinks they know what would constitute their own particular happiness.

There are many pleasures in life to obtain which, people, in their search for joy, will spend time and effort; but which, when possessed, give satisfaction only for the moment. Very soon it will pass away, and they will realize that, after all, the things upon which they had set their hearts have failed to give the happiness they expected, for pleasure is but the shadow of joy, the clouds with which it is covered. And those who spend their lives in its pursuit find themselves, at the end of their search, empty-handed.

There is only one thing that can bring lasting happiness, and it is the same for all, whatever their position in life. But it can never be found by the seekers who think, "I want to find joy, I want to be happy." So long as they think thus, they are lost in the mists of their own illusions and view all things in a false light.

Whosoever would find joy must bring joy to the heart of another. Whosoever would find happiness must make happy those amongst whom one dwells. And herein is a paradox, for no one can give another that which one does not oneself possess. But directly *I* is forgotten in *Thou,* these things are in the power of such a one to bestow, for by this act of self-annihilation— which really means forgetting oneself—one enters into one's kingdom.

21

He that is greatest among you shall be your servant.
—Matthew 23:11

THE practice of humility has always been taught to disciples on the spiritual path by every school of occultism and mysticism, and it is included in all religious systems of instruction. Humility must not, however, be confused with the servility of the hypocrite; and there is a false humility that is far worse than pride. Let the disciple beware. Let the disciple strive to realize the importance of true humility and to separate the real from the false, for, verily, it is the greatest safeguard upon the path. It may be called a magic shield, for all the darts of the evil one may be turned aside by its power.

When anyone begins to tread the path of discipleship, all the instructions and safeguards necessary for the journey are given by the teacher, but often they are not recognized as such by the disciple. So in order to insure their safety, disciples must be tested at every step of the way; for unless they have real knowledge of the perils of the path, they would very soon be overpowered. And there is nothing, not even the sword of strength that can be of greater assistance than the shield of humility. Verily, it is a cover and a refuge in all times of difficulty; and if the surface is kept polished by constant use, the inner meaning of all things will be revealed.

Although humility is the first and the last lesson to be learned upon the spiritual path, it is at the beginning of the journey that it is of the greatest importance as a safeguard. Directly the disciples come in contact with psychic phenomena, they are almost invariably greeted by the dwellers on that plane as "a great soul," and it is suggested to the disciples that they have been chosen to do some important work for the world, which only they are able to do. But woe unto the those who believe these suggestions, for they are all designed to retard one's steps upon the path. Almost everyone will believe a flattering speech about themselves. Very few are able to withstand the idea of being a little further upon the spiritual path than their fellow travelers. This stumbling block is great, and many have been turned from the true path into byways leading to confusion and blindness of vision, oftentimes even to destruction; for nothing has such a power of de-integration as disciples' thoughts of their own greatness. Let them therefore remember the words of Jesus Christ: "Verily I say unto you, whosoever shall not receive the kingdom of God as a little child, shall in no wise enter therein."[1]

1 Luke 18:17.

22

THE connection between spiritual teachers and their disciples is a very subtle thing and easily misunderstood. For while reverence and devotion are naturally given, if these are limited to the personality of the teacher, the spiritual link can never be made. Things of the spirit cannot be translated into physical language and, unless perceived by spiritual vision, cannot even be made intelligible to the mind.

Many of the misunderstandings in the religious world have been caused by attempting to express spiritual verities as physical facts.

There is only one spiritual force, but how it manifests depends upon the channel through which it is expressed, as electricity is one, but in action, it becomes either heat, motive power, destructive force, or (if the channel is a vacuum lamp) light, varying in degree according to the capacity of the lamp.

A teacher who is of God is a powerhouse of spiritual radiance, able to illuminate, according to their receptive capacity, those souls who seek the teacher's guidance. And it is the empty heart, "at leisure from itself,"[1] which can become a lit lamp. In order that the soul may continue to receive illumination, it is, however, an absolute necessity for the link connecting spirit with spirit to remain unbroken. There must be a clear and open path along which the light may travel. It is the work of a disciple to make and maintain such a path, and see to it that no obstruction be deposited thereon. The two essentials needed are faith and trust. Faith in oneself (disciples must be perfectly sure that what they are doing is right for them,

1 Waring, Anna Laetitia, "Father, I Know that All My Life."

even if the whole worlds thinks they are wrong), and trust in the spiritual teacher. Without these two things it is impossible to make the attempt. As a footpath across a field is made by constantly treading it, so a way of communication between teacher and disciple is made by constant concentration. Any obstruction will easily block the way, for it is made by thought and held by thought; therefore if, for instance, a feeling of doubt is allowed an entrance, the spiritual link is weakened.

Although in the end, every soul returns to God, not in every soul is the capacity for the swift ascent by the path of discipleship. It is not those who think they are fit who can become disciples, but those who sincerely desire to become fit, and who are, therefore, willing to place themselves in the attitude of pupil in order that they may understand the lessons taught by life, the teacher of teachers.

23

THOSE who seek a master of wisdom in order to be told the mystery of life will be sent empty away, for even the greatest teacher cannot tell one anything that person does not know, which is a paradox; but truth abides in paradox. A Tibetan mystic has said, "No man can ever be told the truth, which is in him or is not in him. If it is, he will see the truth. If it is not, he will see delusion and will confuse himself with surmise. He who looks for negation beholds it. He who looks for truth beholds negation also but perceives the truth beyond."[1]

A spiritual teacher can impart to a sincere disciple the method of uncovering the truth that is within; for, in the human heart, truth is always more or less deeply buried in error.

When the uncovering is truly and earnestly practiced, the disciple is said to be on the *path of unknowing*, which is the only way to wisdom. This path is set about with many difficulties, and none should attempt to walk thereon except under guidance of one who knows the way; for the unknowing must be a gradual process. No tenet or principle previously held, however erroneous, should be thrown aside until the lesson it can teach has been assimilated. And it must be remembered that the truth of one stage is the error of the next, and the heresy of today is the orthodoxy of tomorrow.

Error must be broken ere the truth it covers can be released, as an eggshell must break to give freedom to the life it contains. And although a shell is of no more use to the bird who

---

1 Mundy, Talbot, *OM: The Secret of Ahbor Valley.*

can soar above its limitations, it was a necessity for the fashioning of its wings; for this reason it should never be broken from without. Only the bird within knows when it is ready to fly, and will itself open the door to freedom.

The unfoldment of wisdom in the human heart is by the growth of one's spiritual vision and cannot be forced. But when the "light of His countenance"[2] shines upon it, it will gently unfold from within, as a rosebud unfolds petal by petal until the heart of the rose lies open to the light of the sun.

When the human heart opens to the sun of righteousness, the whole life becomes illuminated.

2 Psalm 4:6.

24

AS it is said that mere learning will never enable a human being to know God, there is a certain amount of confusion of thought amongst those who aspire to tread the path of seeking, as to what extent the human mind can be used in the search. If knowledge of God cannot be attained through any mental process, then by what means can God be known? For if the reasoning faculty of mind is of no importance on this path, how can one know what one is seeking or recognize it when found, reason being an attribute of mind?.

It is difficult to convey any solution of this question to one who has not realized the supreme mystery of humanity. Seers understand many things of which they cannot speak. To define a truth is to kill it, and the only motive for doing so is that a presentment of a dead fact will sometimes inspire a seeker to search for the living truth.

That which in a human being is striving to realize its origin and essence, is one's innermost being: the soul, or ray of divine light, which is a person's life. All else pertaining to human beings are instruments the soul uses for its expression and experience. The human soul, therefore, uses mind with its reasoning power for the purpose of the search. But although the mind can seek, it cannot find. It can search and uncover everything that is obscure, it can sweep away and destroy every obstacle that stands as a barrier between a person and their God. But to find and see that which the mind has uncovered, another faculty is needed: that of the heart. The mind seeks, the heart finds, for the mystery of God is hidden in itself. "The real abode of God is the heart of man."[1] The key to this problem lies in the fact that the heart cannot see until the mind has accomplished its work of preparation; but when it has done so, it is no longer a necessity in the search. The hands may uncover a treasure, but only the eyes can perceive it.

In the spiritual life of a human being, as in the physical, every faculty must be active, for all are necessary to the life of the whole. Not one must be allowed to remain inactive or unused, but each must be used for the purpose for which it was evolved. The mind cannot do the work of the heart, neither can the heart carry out the functions of the mind.

It is in the right understanding of unity that humanity will find the answer to its questioning.

1 Inayat Khan.

25

THERE is only one truth and one teaching given to aspirants who, by developed intuition, are able to contact the realm of spiritual knowledge. But as there are many degrees of understanding among such souls, their interpretation of it is not one but many; for to faithfully and accurately reproduce such teaching in all its aspects would necessitate perfect knowledge of the language of universal experience—a rare attribute seldom found in a human being. Truth is shown to disciples as a whole; but only so much as they are able, according to their own capacity, to absorb, can be translated into their own mental language. For in order to interpret what the disciples have seen, either to themselves or others, the impression received must be clothed in such words as are contained in a disciple's physical brain. This would necessarily mean that, although the truth perceived is the same in every case, to whatever age, race, or religion the seer may belong, a different interpretation and presentment may be given by each one. Nevertheless, the fundamental essence, which permeates and saturates all wrappings of mental matter, can always be recognized by one who has ever inhaled its fragrance.

26

DIVINE force, when manifested upon the physical plane, is always in a dual aspect and, therefore, capable of being used for good or for evil. The power that creates also destroys. For instance, electricity may be used as a healing power or as a power of destruction. The electricity is the same in both cases, the difference being in its application.

For this reason, the guardians of spiritual power place every kind of obstacle and barrier around and about it, lest human beings, in their ignorance, should destroy themselves. For to have easy access to such a force, without first being prepared by training and discipline to use and control it, would mean disaster to any person. In the hands of the uninitiated, spiritual power is as unsafe as a live electric wire in the hands of a child.

There is grave danger in desiring any kind of spiritual power, however far upon the path one may be. For, if desired with sufficient intensity, one will obtain it. Then woe be unto those if they shall slumber or sleep, for only an unceasing vigilance, beyond the power of most to sustain, will enable them to use it in safety. It will intensify all that is latent within them, which few would have courage to face. Seek not for spiritual powers, O, traveler upon the path. The responsibility is heavy indeed upon those to whom it is entrusted.

27

WHEN a seed of living truth is given from the world of spirit to the material world, the form through which it can come to fruition and multiply must be fashioned from mental matter. It is, therefore, implanted in a human brain. For the initiation of such thought in the physical world, it is necessary, in order that it may be truly uttered, that the human personality chosen to give it birth is prepared by direct contact with those initiating the idea upon the inner planes of being. But when once the thought has been uttered with power or born alive, it then becomes capable of infinite reproduction; and any human brain capable of receiving the impression and making a thought form (i.e., of holding a clear and steady thought) can be used for its spreading, quite irrespective of any other quality it may or may not possess.

This can easily be proved by tracing the evolution of thought. For if any idea, good or evil, is uttered with power, it becomes alive; and there will very soon be millions of people thinking the same thought that came to birth through one human brain.

The nature and quality of impressions received by a person is determined by the color and tuning of one's daily thoughts and habit of life. For no impression of any kind can be received, however impressionable one may be, unless within oneself there is some answering note when the chord is struck.

The method of safeguarding the human mind from all impressions of evil, is daily to tune the heart by the practice of the presence of God: "To enter into thy closet and shut the door."[1] In other words, in the silence of meditation to shut out all else but God, and strive to realize God's presence in the human heart.

1 Matthew 6:6.

28

Thou drawest near in the day that I called upon Thee;
Thou saidst, Fear not."

—*Lamentations 3:57*

THE masters of wisdom have always taught the supreme importance of the mystery of faith, although even their words could not convey to another the inner meaning, which each soul must seek for itself by the light of divine illumination.

Jesus continually tried to teach his disciples how mighty was the power of a faith-full human being. "What things soever ye desire, when ye pray, believe that ye receive them, and ye shall have them."[1]

"If ye have faith as a grain of mustard seed, ye shall say unto this mountain, 'Remove hence to yonder place'; and it shall remove; and nothing shall be impossible unto you." [2]

Saint Paul, to some extent, unveiled the mystery for those who had eyes to see when he said, "Faith is the substance of things hoped for, the evidence of things not seen."[3]

Substance is generally thought of as solid matter having weight and mass, and it is difficult to realize as substance that which cannot be seen by the physical eyes. But if it is thought of in its real meaning, as essence, these words become illuminated.

Faith is the essence of things hoped for. Everything that materializes in the physical world, humans themselves, and every detail of their environment, first has its existence in the

1 Mark 11:24.
2 Matthew 17:20.
3 Hebrews 11:1.

mental sphere, or world of ideas, by creative thought: the things hoped for. But in order that these things may be realized in earthly life, faith is an absolute necessity; for without it, they remain as mental images having no vehicle of expression.

Faith is the substance that makes a material body possible, the stuff from which it is molded. In other words, when the note of faith is sounded, the physical atoms that are needed to form a body of materialization will group themselves according to the positive call, or vibration, of faith. For faith is the magnet that draws the things hoped for from the unmanifested to the world of manifestation: the evidence of things not seen. "The man of perfect faith can extend his influence to inanimate things and disembodied spirits; he can move heaven and earth . . . without encountering any hindrance."[4] Faith is the open door through which all blessings can come; but when the door is closed by doubt, then although the blessing is waiting outside, it cannot be received.

4 Lieh Tzu, *Taoist Teachings from the Book of Lieh Tzu.*

29

"ESOTERIC training," "occult training," are phrases frequently heard from the lips of those who are generally ignorant of their real meaning.

There are thousands of books written upon this subject, and thousands of teachers quite ready to give instruction and training. But those who are thus trained are no further upon the path than they were before, however much knowledge they appear to possess.

It is not in this way that the great masters of wisdom deal with an earnest soul who has asked for instruction upon the path to God. Their method is much more simple and takes place almost entirely in the inner life; and because so simple, is thought by many to be of so little importance that they seek teachers who will give them various difficult tests and kinds of training. Did they but know it, the tests given by the great ones to their pupils are far more searching and final, although unknown to the candidate, who is unconscious of being tested; and they are given in the ordinary life of the world, for life itself is the real initiator. Often they consist of such things as the disciple's attitude to fellow humans or to duties and responsibilities; whether the rhythm of one's life is harmonious; and again, in service, so seldom recognized as a test and yet one that no true disciple can evade. "Service is an essential duty for the disciple. Its gains are superior to those of worship."[1]Many think service means to serve God in great things, perhaps to give up all their worldly possessions. And

1 Sharaf al-Din Maneri, *Letters from a Sufi Teacher.*

they feel quite ready to do this but fail to realize that possibly ordinary uninteresting work, even routine work in daily life, may be required of them; and that in some apparently unimportant detail they are being trained and tested. The real test of service is to be always ready to serve, wherever service may be required, in however lowly a capacity. For it is not the quality or importance of the service given that is the test; it is the quick, spontaneous response of the disciple to the call for help in any direction.

Knowledge of occult or hidden truths is not given for the asking. The disciples must first make themselves worthy by service to stand before God.

> *Seek the knowledge that is revealed by service,*
> *and seek the service that is revealed by knowledge.*
> *—Khwaja Hasan al-Basri*

30

TO the eyes of the soul, religion appears as matter and truth as spirit. Some form of body is necessary to contain truth in a material world. And to those who are not yet able to receive the vision of imperishable things, the religious form that truth uses to veil herself appears as the only reality. They do not realize that it can only appear as reality while being worn by truth; and even although she may wear the veils of seventy thousand warring sects, it would still be truth beneath them all, wearing each one for a different purpose, as a person may wear many special robes for special occasions yet still remain the same under them all.

The garment worn by truth while dwelling in the physical world is a coat of many colors, woven of every colored thread known to and recognizable by humans, in order that they may see truth; for their eyes would be blinded by the unveiled dazzling light of its white purity, which cannot be perceived save by those who have the open vision. The colors represent the various religious faiths and teachings that have, from time to time, been brought to the world—in every age a message suitable to the color of the human mind—and this has given rise to untold bitterness, hatred, and strife. For when aspirants are searching for truth, they are so constituted that, until the inner eyes are open, they can only perceive one color in the robe they wear and, therefore, cannot believe that any other color than the one seen can possibly be visible to another. This has been the tragedy of religion since the beginning of the world. If a person would try to see with the eyes of another, or at any rate to admit that what appears to one as red may to another view be green (since both are but appearances), the inner vision would begin to unfold until that person could see with the eyes of all humanity. Then would the horizon widen, and the realization come that all colors were needed to make the white light of living truth.

What does it matter upon what religious path one seeks one's God, so long as one does seek God? And how can humanity, with its puny comprehension of eternal truths, limit God, the All-Living, the All-Comprehending, to one way and one path, when all paths are God's; and all, if followed in sincerity, must lead to God: the one goal to which all humanity is traveling. "However men approach Me, even so do I welcome them, for the path men take from every side is Mine, O, Partha."[1]

It is true that one path may be more suitable to some than to others. That will always be so, and applies to physical as well as spiritual life; but it is great presumption upon the part of a person to assume that one's way to God is better than any other. For that person, yes, it may be so, or naturally one would not walk thereon; but one should not attempt to control and, much less, to condemn the way chosen by another. By so doing, a person is usurping to oneself a power not used by God, Who, having created humans in God's Own image, gave them the birthright of free will.

This is the secret of the persecutions and the wars fought in the name of religion: a human being, by coercing another, is acting against the law of God; for coercion is a disintegrating force and can never help any soul to realize unity, where alone reality abides.

By this, of course, it is not meant that people should not help others to seek God; for although none may be coerced, they may be shown the beauty of the path of wisdom and the ease with which the journey may be accomplished by treading it. But those who are giving their lives for this purpose, before embarking upon their mission, should have some measure

1 Bhagavad Gita.

of understanding of *what* is God; and where and how God may be found; and a realization of the mystic teaching that every path is God's path; and by whatsoever one a person may travel, however winding, difficult, crooked, or straight it may be, at the end of the path one has chosen to tread, one will meet one's God.

31

Render therefore unto Caesar the things which are Caesar's, and unto God the things that are God's.

—Matthew 22:21

IN these words of the Master there is given, to those who have ears to hear, the instructions necessary for treading the path trodden by all those who have attained perfection.

So many people think that to follow the path of the mystic it is essential to leave altogether the life of the world and think only of God. This, of course, in one sense is true; and when the disciple knows what God really is, the disciple will understand and realize the inner meaning known to those who have found God, but that can only be comprehended when the eyes of the soul are fully open.

When the Christ has been born in a human heart, then the whole horizon becomes filled with God; the eyes can behold only God, Who is all that exists; and nothing whatsoever can exist bereft of God, because all things and beings are part of the One Life. But in the human life, subject to the law of duality, there are two aspects: the inner and the outer. And the reason of all the confusion of thought is that the human being divides these, which in reality are one, into two separate periods of time, assigning the inner life as belonging to God and the things of God, and the outer to the world and all it means of earthly life. In order to reach the perfection enjoined by Jesus, these two aspects, known to Sufis as *jelal* and *jemal*, must be realized simultaneously. Whosoever can do this has reached the stage known as *master* (i.e., one who has attained mastery). A master can hold all things, but cannot be held by any. Life and death, as known to the dweller upon earth, have no meaning for the master, for the master has conquered both and understands that all evil is inverted good. The master's physical body lives the ordinary human life, but the master's soul dwells always in the presence of God. And because of this, a master views the outer life as a garment God wears to veil the mystery of the Godhead; a garment woven from God's own Self, as the silkworm spins a cocoon of silken thread in which to hide and shield the life until the hour of its fulfillment.

Thus a master understands, without a shadow of doubt, that all things rendered unto Caesar are in reality rendered unto God, for in very truth, Caesar and all he stands for, as well as all things whatsoever, can have no existence apart from God, in Whom all live and move, and have their being.

Masters can experience anything they desire to experience, and they have the power to hold all things. But if they were to retain any beyond its allotted time, the experience would hold them, and they would lose their mastery.

Therefore, the lives of the great ones are a continual balance and adjustment, and a rendering to Caesar the things that are Caesar's and to God the things that are God's.

When in any life there is a disharmony, it is because this at-one-ment has not been realized. Something has been neglected, either in the inner life or in the outer. For to obtain equilibrium or perfect balance, the duties of both must be equally discharged, for neither the things belonging to Caesar nor those belonging to God may be neglected.

Whosoever has discovered the inner truth of this mystery knows that the fulfillment of every desire possible for a human being to conceive is to be found in God alone, Who is the completion of every soul's desire.

32

In the currents of life, in action's storm,
I wander and I wave,
Everywhere I be!
Birth and the grave,
An infinite sea,
A web ever growing,
A life every glowing;
Thus at time's whizzing loom I spin,
And weave the living vesture
That God is mantled in.

— *Johann Wolfgang von Goethe*

THE whole manifested universe, with its myriad forms of life from atom to angel, is the living garment of God: that by which God may be known.

Known by and to God, while dwelling in the human heart, God's highest expression this material world, in which, made in the image of God, humanity is evolving into that likeness, or oneness. Every living thing—and nothing exists devoid of life—therefore, all things and all beings, are only things and beings by virtue of belonging to and partaking of the life of the One and Only Being, called by various names in different lands, but known to all as the supreme God, without Whom nothing could live that does live.

"From the Unmanifested, all the manifested streams forth at the coming of day; at the coming of night they dissolve ever in that called the Unmanifested."[1]

1 Bhagavad Gita.

As the river seeks the sea, where losing its identity as river it becomes sea, even so does humanity seek God. Or, in other words, God seeks God. God Immanent in the divine Creation, seeking God Transcendent; the part seeking the whole that it may be united with it.

Humanity can only find God by knowledge of the garment God wears, called by mystics *the divine wisdom*, through which, when a seeker has mastered and assimilated it, the seeker may obtain a vision of the hidden God. "The knowledge of the Creator follows from the knowledge of created objects."[2] The only way human beings can approach God is by an understanding of the veils, their numberless forms, colors, and sounds with which God covers the Divine Self in the material world; for God unveiled, no one could gaze upon and remain in a physical body. Such an illumination would shatter all form, which, prematurely returning to the ethers from which it came forth, would prevent the human soul from fulfilling its allotted task.

Humanity seeks God and the knowledge of God in all kinds of strange and inaccessible places, by difficult and subtle paths, even trying by the power of occult arts to wrest from nature the hidden secret of existence. But God will never be found of such seekers. God, the Ever Present, dwells close to humans in the life of every day. For in truth, God is all-pervading in the outer as in the inner life: "The One and the manifold everywhere present."[3]

"Human! Know thyself," is the mystic teaching given down the ages by all prophets, seers, saints, and masters to their pupils and disciples. When this mystery is realized, the secret of God, the proof of God, and the knowledge of God may all be found within the human being. And no matter what may be one's environment, it is possible to live in the constant realization of the presence of God, for verily, God is the very Self of all beings.

2 Sharaf al-Din Maneri, *Letters From a Sufi Teacher.*

3 Bhagavad Gita.

33

Blessed is the man that heareth Me, watching daily at My gates, waiting at the posts of My doors. For whoso findeth Me findeth life.

—*Proverbs 8:34–35*

THE disciple who would meditate upon God and who desires to realize the presence of God, should understand that this condition cannot be attained by effort, for effort blocks the mind, rendering it unreceptive.

When God visits the heart, it is always when one has stilled the mind; in other words, has rendered oneself negative, or receptive to God. For unless one is in the attitude to receive, God cannot enter.

Meditation or silence must be effortless and natural, and should give a feeling of rest and peace, which is revivifying and exhilarating to all the bodies: spiritual, mental, and physical. This meditation is for the purpose of receiving newness of life, God's life, which in this way is received in such full measure that it overflows and enriches the life of all those with whom the recipient comes in contact. It must not be confused with concentration, which demands a positive attitude and is a different process.

When, after a silence or meditation, there is any feeling of strain or tiredness, it is because the negative condition, necessary to enable a human being to approach the courts of God, has not been realized.

34

THERE are quite a number of people on earth today who profess to be living the inner life, or life of the spirit, because they are able to prove by demonstration to others their possession of some unusual power or knowledge. And although it is very easy in this way to make the majority believe someone's claim to spirituality, for even that person can be deceived by their own claim to be considered great, a truly spiritual person can always be recognized by one whose eyes are open to behold the things of the spirit; and such an one would never mistake the false for the true.

Whoever claims to possess spiritual power are false claimants whose feet have not touched even the threshold of reality. Alas! They are building around their souls a prison house of their own thoughts about themselves, from which they can never escape until self has been annihilated.

The lips of those who really know are sealed by their knowledge, and although they make no claim to be different from others, in the inner life they know and are known.

These are the blessed ones of God, whose presence is a blessing and a benediction. For they live in the constant realization of God's presence, where *I* ceases to be.

35

A HUMAN being is a complete miniature of God and God's universe. In humanity are heaven and hell and the whole hierarchy: love that creates, and love that sustains; the creative force and all the pairs of opposites; also the five elements, which compose the heavens and the earth and all that is in them.

Whosoever understands one's own self, verily, knows all things.

"So God created man in His own image, in the image of God created He him; male and female created He them."[1] Positive and negative are two parts of one whole, and neither is complete without the other.

The whole manifestation is part of the one God. God is positive, humanity is negative; although when united, there is, in reality, neither positive nor negative. But the result of such a union is beyond comprehension by the human mind. "Union exists beyond all thought and speech, between great Allah and the soul of each."[2] Spirit and matter are one, not two; but in order to create a universe, part of spirit solidifies itself. Thus becoming limited to time and space, it forms what, to humanity, is known as matter. As human beings are located in matter, living in a world of matter, it is difficult for them to realize this oneness; they think of spirit and matter as two distinct conditions, one opposed to the other. It is true that matter is the opposite of spirit, but it is the opposite aspect of itself, not something apart and antagonistic to it. While

1 Genesis 1:27.

2 Jalal ad-Din Rumi.

humans, by their thoughts, keep these two aspects separate and disconnected, they can never know the mystery of oneness.

Spirit is the real human self, with which one should strive to identify oneself.

Matter is an appearance in time.

When the small self can be lost in God, then will one know oneself.

36

We are no other than a moving row
Of magic shadow-shapes that come and go
Round with the sun-illumin'd lantern held
In midnight by the Master of the Show.[1]

—*Omar Khayyam*

IF the master of the show is thought of as God, the arbitrary controller of one's destiny, it is natural that one should resent such a conception. But if a person can think of the master as the innermost being, or human soul, a different light is thrown upon the many parts played by one player through many lives or in one life. Those who are slaves of time could view various experiences, however terrible, that occurred in the long ago, with equanimity, although they might be unable to understand the reason for similar experiences in a life of today. But those who have risen above the limits of time would realize that, to a soul who has great capacity for absorbing experiences, it would be a necessity to take a different part in many plays, even in one lifetime; although not one of them is the real self of the actor who, having ceased to identify with the experiences and taking one's true place as spectator, becomes master of the show. And the reason for the play is understood.

Such ones can now watch many characters, which were expressions of their outer selves, unfold before their view as a cinema will unfold the story of a player. They can watch

1 Omar Khayyam, *The Rubaiyat*, trans. Edward Fitzgerald (London: Quaritch, 1896).

the play from beginning to end and know that it was all as a dream before the soul.

The essence of every experience, good or bad, which has been lived through and finished, remains as atmosphere surrounding the soul until the end of its journey as a human being. This forms a medium through which the light of the soul can be received and focused upon those still in darkness. But while anything more than pure essence remains, the atmosphere is cloudy and thick, which prevents a person from receiving or imparting to others, the light of God.

It must not be forgotten that a human soul obtains its strength from evil, according to its power of resistance. Therefore, experience of the pairs of opposites is a necessity to one who would attain to mastery on the path.

The soul takes two journeys: the outer one, whose goal is physical manifestation; and the inner, or return journey, whose goal is God.

In the outward journey it draws round itself cover upon cover of experiences, which make it separate and distinct from every other soul.

The return journey consists of putting off these covers, one by one.

To return by the path of ignorance means that each cover over the soul is broken from without by the hand of destiny, through the storms and buffetings of life, causing much pain and suffering. But wisdom teaches that each cover may be gently unloosed from within, with knowledge that, for every one thus loosed, there is greater freedom for the soul until the last cover falls away and the essence of all experience remains as atmosphere, or what is called personality, throughout the whole of that soul's human life. This is the way of wisdom trodden by the mystics. And when they have become masters of the path, they can cause any experience to cover their souls, and dissolve it at will. Then no experience of any kind, good or bad, has any power over them; but its essence pervades the whole life as a subtle perfume, which attracts all. Many try to obtain this by surrounding themselves with all the beautiful things of life, but the secret is known only to those who have mastered themselves, and lies in a peculiar blend of essences extracted from strange places.

A student of the alchemy of nature will be able, to some extent, to realize this by meditating upon the essence of attar of roses.

When a gardener wishes to produce perfect roses, after planting the tree where it can receive the light of the sun, the gardener will water and prune it, and place around its roots a quantity of manure.

The action of manure, when in contact with the tree, causes increased growth, resulting in perfect flowers from which the essence of perfume can be distilled. This subtle beauty may be called the personality of the rose.

What can be told to those who have ears to hear such truths, is that what the world calls *goodness* cannot of itself produce the fragrance of personality, which has a charm, conscious or unconscious, for all who come within its influence.

37

A QUESTION frequently upon the lips of humans is, "What or Who is God, and where can I find God?" How can a limited human being, so infinitesimal a part of such a mighty whole, comprehend in any degree the Omnipotent, Omnipresent One, Creator of humanity and of angels, or restrict to one particular place the God that dwells in all and through all and Who is all? As well might the fishes ask, "Who or what is the ocean, and where can it be found?" or a molecule of the human body cry, "Who or what is a human being, and how can I reach it?"

And yet it is natural that people should seek to know the source of their being, the ultimate end of the whole humanity; only what must be remembered, is that the Only Being cannot be known through the brain. The only way that God can ever become a reality to humans is through the heart. "To analyze God is to dethrone God."[1] The brain is analytical: it dissects and classifies. The heart is synthetic; therefore, in moments of ecstasy or upliftment, when the consciousness is raised above material things, it, as it were, senses the truth of the existence of God and knows that "Closer is He than breathing, and nearer than hands and feet."[2]

It is true these are but momentary glimpses granted to humans in order that they may, even while living the ordinary daily life of difficulties, disappointments, and failures, have a sure and certain knowledge that life as a whole is working

1 Inayat Khan, *The Bowl of Saki.*

2 Tennyson, Alfred, "The Higher Pantheism."

towards a known and destined goal, although the purpose is beyond their understanding.

Those great ones who are masters upon the path have tuned their hearts to be always in tune with the divine chord of love, harmony, and beauty. They are able to respond to every note that vibrates when the winds of God breathe upon those living harps. And when the hand of God touches the heart-strings, harmonious melody floods the whole atmosphere, so that not only they themselves, but all those who are within reach of their influence, become conscious in the depths of their being, although sometimes unconscious upon the surface, of the presence of the living God.

38

Oh that I knew where I might find Him! That I might come even to His seat!

—Job 23:3

THE only answer that can be given to humanity's eternal questions, "What is God" and "Where may God be found?" is that "God is love; and he that dwelleth in love dwelleth in God, and God in him."[1] Whoever is able to experience love's highest expression will know as much of God as it is possible for a human mind to know. Love is the bridge over which humanity passes from mortality to immortality.

When the mystic writers speak of God dwelling in the human heart and use such phrases as "until Christ be formed in you"[2]; "No man hath seen God at any time. If we love one another, God dwelleth in us"[3]; and the reply of Jesus to the Pharisees: "The kingdom of God is within you"[4]; it is God as love of which they are speaking. To love, all things are possible, for power, creative force, beauty, and harmony are all attributes of love. When it fully awakes in any human heart (this quickening is always through pain and sacrifice), such an one is called *God-like* or *Christ-like.*

In the ancient schools of mysticism and in the teachings of the Egyptian mysteries, the injunction given to every candidate was, "Know thyself"; for there, uncovered before the eyes of the seer, will be found the secret of God.

1 1 John 4:16.

2 Galatians 4:19.

3 1 John 4:12.

4 Luke 17:21.

Those who can comprehend the symbology of the teaching contained in the first chapter of Genesis can see the unfoldment of the mystery of manifestation. "And God said, 'Let us make man in Our image, after Our likeness. . . .' "So God created man in His own image; male and female, created He them."[5]

If this teaching can be approached in a lowly and reverential spirit, one may try to imagine that the One Only Being, the Unmanifest, in order to become manifest and express Its many aspects, created from Itself a universe; or, as it is said, "The One willed to multiply"[6] an infinite variety of worlds for the purpose of giving expression to every aspect of the Godhead, of which humanity can have no shadow of comprehension.

Adam—humanity created in the image of God, and therefore a microcosm of the macrocosm—produced from his own body the form by which and through which love, the seed of divinity within humanity, could be brought to fruition and be expressed in manifold forms; for there can be no expression of love without an embodiment. Therefore, for the purpose of manifestation, duality is necessary: positive and negative, jelal and jemal, lover and beloved. Thus the One becoming two forms a trinity: love, lover, and beloved. From the action and reaction of these pairs of opposites is born the result: infinite reproduction of form to hold the One Life; and in every form thus created, the seed of the Godhead, love in embryo, can be traced. For the need of love is a universal experience, and although the human soul, blinded by the illusion of its identification with form, vainly pursues love in strange guises and through devious ways, in reality, through all its phases, it is humanity seeking God, however unconscious the mind may be of the soul's true purpose.

It is impossible to conceive the glory, majesty, power, and might of the One God. Neither are there words in any language by

5 Genesis 1:26–27.

6 Chandogya Upanishad.

which an idea can be conveyed, except as a cover, for the reality that cannot be told.

So to continue in the halting and inadequate speech of humanity: to every planet its own rhythm and tuning. To the dwellers upon earth, God can only be known through God's love aspect. "For love is of God; and every one that loveth is born of God, and knoweth God. He that loveth not knoweth not God, for God is love."[7]

Then it is realized how infinitesimal a part is this planet in the great universe of myriad worlds, solar systems, planets, and stars innumerable, each of which has its own rhythmic purpose in the divine plan; and that this law of becoming, embodiment, and re-becoming is imposed upon every atom through the whole manifestation, whether forming worlds or molecules. Angels and principalities, or germs and worms—how is it possible that one human being could ever hope to understand, by any mental process, the Creator of All?

As the river seeks its source to become one with the ocean of which it is a part, so humanity, either consciously or unconsciously, is seeking God, Who is its source and origin. But humanity, as part of God, obviously cannot find God by trying to understand God. Can the part have knowledge of the whole? To analyze a thing, one must be apart from it, not of it.

According to the measure of one's ability to lose consciousness of self, so one will gain consciousness of God, when all questioning will cease in God-realization. But the human soul can only fully realize God through the at-one-ment of God-identification, where consciousness of self, as a separate being, ceases. Love is lost in the beloved, and humanity re-becomes God.

7 1 John 4:7–8.

39

IN reality, everyone is seeking the love of God, by whatever name they call it and by whatever strange path they seek it. Even one who denies the existence of God is still seeking God, although unconscious of the seeking.

Divine love is a magnet that attracts all beings and things, whatsoever, to itself. The person does not exist whom nothing attracts. Everyone is conscious of some unsatisfied desire, which they try to appease by every kind of gratification of the outer senses; but in the end this leaves them more and more unsatisfied, for nothing short of perfection, which is God, can wholly satisfy the human soul, from Whom it came and to Whom it must return.

It is not only humanity that is seeking God. Everything that has life seeks life, the source of its existence. A Sufi sage has said, "Should thy inner eyes unfold, every atom would tell thee a hundred secrets. Then wouldst thou see each atom ever advancing. All are absorbed in the march—thou art blind—and the march goes on in thee as well. There is no limit to the progress of love. . . . From the highest heaven to the lower abyss, all things are seeking and striving."[1]

It is an absolute necessity that those who aspire to tread the path should understand the meaning of unity and see, by the light of divine wisdom, the oneness of life. No one can live to themselves alone. Each person's every action affects the whole, of which that person is a part. One can neither reach heaven nor descend into hell alone. Others travel with one,

1 Sharaf al-Din Maneri, *Letters From a Sufi Teacher*. Letter 53.

partaking of one's joy and sorrow. In whatever condition one finds oneself, thousands must also suffer or rejoice through that one person.

The whole earth, viewed from the divine outlook, is one unit evolving towards its perfection through the countless millions of living and breathing creatures forming the various kingdoms of nature belonging to it; all of which, including the human, form one body and are its means of expression.

If one atom refuses its appointed task, the whole becomes disorganized; just as in the physical body revolutionary cells will cause malignant growths, by which the whole body suffers. Our planet itself is one of a group of planets revolving round a sun through which they receive light and life. Even the sun is part of a greater group still. But through all stars, planets, solar systems, and universes, one law is observed, one life sustains, and there is but one goal to which all are journeying.

40

LIFE is light, and light is eternal. That which obscures light is its own shadow. When night falls upon the Earth, light has not died; but the Earth has changed its position, has, as it were, turned its back to the light and is only conscious of darkness. The light has not changed, it is eternally the same; but to realize this, the Earth must turn round.

What should be taught today is the unity and indestructibility of all life.

The world in which we live is but the outer, or exoteric expression, of one great organism. There are many others, and every particle of life upon the globe is part of the whole and necessary to it. The living atoms, be they molecules of matter in the human body, or a complete human being, who is an atom in that mighty whole, are continually moving from one place to another. They do not remain stationary, but change of place or expression does not mean cessation of life.

When a person is able to emerge from the outermost, or physical, body, those who are still in that condition call that person dead, because the person has passed beyond their limited comprehension. Solid matter is limiting; and human beings, while encased in a covering composed of that matter, are limited to its rate of vibration as water is limited by the condition of ice, unless and until they know the secret of vibrations, which will enable them to transcend its limitation even while remaining in a physical body. "The world is overcome—Aye! even here! By such as fix their faith on unity."[1]

1 Bhagavad Gita, trans. Edwin Arnold. (Courier Corp. 1899).

The law of creation is duality. A physical body is created and subject to birth and death, but the real human self, the soul or spirit, is not created and, therefore, cannot know death. "Death hath not touched it at all, dead though the house of it seems!."[2]

> *Nay! But as when one layeth*
> *His worn-out robes away,*
> *And, taking new ones, sayeth,*
> *"These will I wear today!"*
> *So, putteth by the spirit,*
> *Lightly, its garb of flesh,*
> *And passeth to inherit*
> *A residence afresh.*
>
> —*Bhagavad Gita*

The law of spirit is unity, oneness; it knows no opposite or opposing force. While humans identify themselves with body, they know death; but when they can identify themselves with spirit, they know only life, and for these there is no death. The person who is freed from earthly body is no more dead than a butterfly is dead that has emerged from the caterpillar and chrysalis condition. One has but changed one's world or changed one's condition, that life may have more freedom of expression. Physical matter forms the densest and most solid of all the robes the soul wears during its journey, and offers the greatest resistance to control. For this reason, divine illumination, or the vision of God, when attained in the physical body, is the final victory over self.

2 Ibid.

41

Let your virtues dissolve in the sea of purity.[1]

—Inayat Khan

IF the soul cannot be touched by its experience but remains always the same, why should people try to acquire virtues? What do they matter?

Virtues do not belong to the soul, they are not attributes but the means by which it is liberated; in other words, the material from which the human soul fashions wings, which will enable it, at will, to soar to the highest heaven and also to remain on earth or descend into hell. In its fundamental essence the soul is always the same. It cannot change, but during the journey it is held captive in matter until, as a human being, it can achieve its own freedom, which can only be gained by control or mastery of all that lies below its own level. If the mind is negative to the soul, or the Divine Self within, the gates are opened, and one is free to pass in and out. But if, on the other hand, the mind assumes a positive attitude towards the things of the spirit, refusing to become "as a little child," it draws around the soul a solid wall of mental matter, thus forming a prison house that holds it to the earth.

Virtues, in themselves, are of no importance; but the practice of them is an absolute necessity for the soul's liberation from all the bodies belonging to human beings, which does not imply that a person will have them or cease to live upon earth. When Jesus, after his crucifixion, descended into hell, it was by his own free will; but before he did so he had him-

1 Inayat Khan, *Vadan*.

self, as a human being, mastered hell by voluntarily experiencing it. His prayer to the Father, "If it be possible, let this cup pass from me; nevertheless, not my will, but Thy will be done,"[2] shows his humanity surrendering itself, or being negative to, the divine will. The cup did not pass from him until it was empty. He, the Blessed One, drank the contents, meaning that they became part of himself. Nothing was spared him. His nearest disciples slept during his hour of agony and deserted him, Every indignity was placed upon him, and he was condemned to die the death of a common malefactor; but the uttermost depth of hell must have been reached to call forth from him who realized his oneness with the Father, the cry, "My God, My God, why hast Thou forsaken me?"[3] But at that moment, when he felt that even God had forsaken him, he also touched the highest heaven and conquered earth and hell.

After this he could walk through the deepest hell, untouched and unmoved, to free the spirits in prison.

2 Matthew 26:39.

3 Matthew 27:46.

42

IT is difficult to express in earthly terms the inner meaning of life or to explain nature's secrets. There is a point where joy and sorrow, and all the other pairs of opposites, meet and become neither one nor the other. But this mystery cannot be explained in words and can only be fully understood by one who is a master of paradox.

In the teaching of the Sufis, the secret of paradox is to be found in a right understanding of *jelal*, *jemal*, and *kemal*, which are expressed upon the physical plane as *positive*, *negative*, and *neutral*.

The law governing the world, upon which humanity is evolving, is duality; and in consequence of this law, humans cannot know or understand anything apart from its opposite. The soul, as a human being, cannot experience heaven or hell unless it also knows their opposites. If one could, one would cease to be human, and become either angel or devil. The one who would reach the heights must have knowledge of the depths. Jesus, as perfect human, ere he ascended to his Father, experienced the uttermost depths; but it is not given to every person to ascend unto the heights, nor to plumb the deeps of life. Only the great souls who have mastered life have attained to this power.

The inner meaning of the pairs of opposites is revealed to one who has experienced ecstasy, that state of perfection wherein the two meet and become one, which is the moment of the soul's illumination. "For he is our peace, who hath made both one, and hath broken down the middle wall of partition."[1] When the positive and negative poles of electricity are brought together upon the physical plane, light is produced wherever a lamp is made ready to receive it.

When, in the human being, the positive and negative poles are united upon the spiritual plane, a person receives divine illumination. But this cannot be allowed to happen until one has learned the control of all one's bodies, physical, emotional, and mental, and mastered the laws that govern them.

The secret, or inner meaning, of life must be approached with great reverence. It is one of the veils under which God hides, and may not be drawn aside for the gratification of the curious.

The wise have said, "Do not search for a mystery that can be hidden by human beings. Seek the mystery within yourself." When you have found God within your heart, all mysteries whatsoever will be uncovered. "For there is nothing covered, that shall not be revealed; neither hid, that shall not be known."[2]

---

1 Ephesians 2:14.

2 Luke 12:2.

43

TRAVELERS upon the path of return are frequently puzzled by the many difficulties and bewilderments they meet upon the way. Some even feel discouraged and lose faith in themselves or in their guide, for no one can tread the return path unless guided by one who has traversed it and is, therefore, able to guide others. No one should seek this guidance except from a spiritual teacher in whom one has complete confidence, and if one can trust that teacher's knowledge of the path.

Not everyone who aspires can become a disciple. The teacher can help an aspirant, can ensure the aspirant a safe journey; but the teacher cannot tread the path for the aspirant.

A Sufi sage has said, "If the spirit of the path lies latent in a candidate, it will unfold by his (the teacher's) company and service. The divine law works in this way."[1]

The essence of this teaching is in the word *service*. Many seek a spiritual teacher for help in their daily life, for consolation, for healing, for deliverance from difficulties, for the unfoldment of power; and a few only for guidance and help in their search for God. A true teacher will give to each one, whether worthy or unworthy, what the seeker asks; but the result of the teacher's gift depends upon the sincerity of the recipient and whether the spirit of giving or of taking is the more active within the seeker. The generous heart is always anxious to serve, and true service—not work seen of people, which is frequently for the glorification of the personality,

1 Sharaf al-Din Maneri, *Letters From a Sufi Teacher*.

but service at the secret altar, unseen and unknown by others—will take a traveler very far upon the path of return to God, and will be of the greatest help in taking the traveler safely through the many difficulties that beset one; for there is no room for fear in a heart filled with desire to serve. A real server, therefore, is able to walk safely through many dangerous places, often unconscious of the danger until it is past. When such an one, with heart athirst for God, seeks the guidance of a master of the path, realization of many truths will come.

44

Raise the stone and there thou shalt find Me;
cleave the wood and there am I.
—*Henry Van Dyke, after* The Gospel of Thomas

THE center, or positive electrically charged nucleus, seemed perfectly still, circular in form and in appearance rather dark. Surrounding this were apparently thousands of minute particles in perpetual movement, their form resembling very thin spirals, in appearance suggesting living, moving light, very bright. Although all were in constant and rapid motion, they remained at a fixed distance from the center, which they surrounded on every side, forming a circle. The center was never touched by one of these. The only way they can be described, although very inadequately, is as tiny, intensely active spirals of living light, giving the impression of life itself. No particular color was noticeable, yet all colors seemed faintly suggested. The impression received was that it would be quite impossible for them to be anything except fully alive. But although possessed of eternal life, being in themselves life, light, and motion, nothing could be accomplished or created except by their obedience to the law of rhythm, by answering to the keynote of the vibratory chord to which they belong, the positive magnetic call of their own group center, or group soul.

The positively charged nucleus holds the pattern, rejecting those particles not belonging to its group by the rhythm of its motion; and the negative electrons take their appointed places around that nucleus or center.

It is almost impossible to describe in words that will in any degree express the reality; but although their arrangement was according to an unalterable plan, no particular electron ever remained stationary. All were interchangeable and equal, having no separate or individual personality (this belonged to the atom as a whole). The important thing was that there should always be the same number, in exactly the same arrangement. Although all were in perpetual activity, being themselves life, they could not remain still.

It may be inferred from this that, because the positive center has the appearance of immobility, it is therefore not life; but that would be an error. The truth is that a positively electrified nucleus is in such extraordinary rapid motion that its appearance, even to clairvoyant vision, is one of utter stillness. A seer, however, whose eyes were open to the inner vision of divine knowledge, could view the intense activity of these rapid vibrations and could see that each separate negative electron was held in place by invisible lines of magnetic force coming from the center, which was, in very truth, the source and substance of the life in which, and round which, they "lived and moved and had their being"[1] as an atom. The seer could watch certain numbers of completed atoms (i.e., positively charged nuclei with their complement, or negative charge) collectively obeying a higher vibratory call, becoming negative to that positive note and, forming themselves around it, becoming what is termed a molecule. These again, in turn, obeying their own positive call, uniting to form mineral, vegetable, or animal bodies; the number and arrangement of the molecules depending upon the particular form and function they were to express. Of this substance is molded the physical embodiment of all created things and beings. A seed may become a positive nucleus when the outer covering breaks by being buried in the earth. After death and burial in the darkness, it rises towards the light and is then able to

1 Acts 17:28,

draw around itself, or attract, the molecules that are negative to its positive charge of vegetable life. And, in earthly language, the seed becomes a plant.

This process is repeated throughout the whole manifested universe. Each group, in turn, obeying the rhythmic law imposed upon all from the highest to the lowest, becomes positive to that which is below it, and negative to that which is above and to which it is being inevitably up-drawn. The whole held together and in its appointed place by one positive life force working downwards through all forms, and to which all are negative. One life, one law, one goal: the Only Being from Whom all came and to Whom all must return when the call sounds.

On the return path, positive becomes negative, and negative, positive. The negative must seek and be united with the positive note to which it is in tune. This is illustrated by the fact that in the musical scale each note in turn is flat, or negative, to the note above it; and sharp, or positive, to that which is below it.

The law of attraction and repulsion works throughout the universe, from chemical affinities to the stars in their courses. "In every atom slumbers the might of the Self."[2]

In different ages various names have been given for the beginning of physical life. To the mystic it is known as *the rhythmic breath of God*. This is the One Living Substance from which all things whatsoever are made, and upon every minutest particle of which is stamped the whole plan and structure of every form. Also, the law of government of every group or community is impressed upon each atom forming a group, whether molecule, state, nation, planet, or solar system. It is only by obedience to the rhythmic law that any group as a whole, or its units individually, can exist harmoniously. "Each atom doth invisibly enshrine the deep-veiled

2 Iqbal, Muhammad, *The Secrets of the Self: A Philosophical Poem*, trans. by Reynold A. Nicholson (London: Macmillan, 1920).

beauty of the soul divine."[3] If there is any divergence from this law, any weakness in the center of a group, be it atom, nation, planet, or a human being, it is possible for part of the negative charge, which can only be held in place by the positive note being in tune (meaning negative to that which is above and positive to that which is below) to break away from its center; and in so doing, form itself into an, as it were, false center, and attempt independent government. As this is an interruption of the rhythm, disharmony is at once apparent; and in time, unless adjusted, the whole group will disintegrate.

In the cells of the human body this results in malignant growths such as cancer; in a state or nation, in anarchy; and it affects not only itself but other groups, both above and below it.

The spirit, or essence, of matter is light; and even in the densest form it is capable of being raised from the solid, through the liquid, gaseous, and etheric states, to its original condition of spirit-matter. But of this mystery of transmutation more may not be written. "Know thou that matter and spirit are both without beginning."[4]

At the outbreathing (jelal) of God, the Only Being, countless millions of tiny living entities come into manifestation, separate, and group according to plan, into form after form. The One becomes many.

At God's inbreathing (jemal), the many become One.

Then is a period of rest (kemal) until once again a manifestation is outbreathed, for perhaps a fuller expression. But the purpose of God and what lies beyond cannot be grasped by the mind, and may not be unveiled by the human hand. Only in the deepest reverence may this thought be approached.

> *I am the source of the forthgoing of the whole universe and likewise the place of its dissolving. There is naught whatso-*

3 Mahmud ibn Abd al-Karim Shabistari, *The Mystic Rose Garden.*

4 Bhagavad Gita.

ever higher than I, O Dhanañjaya. All this is threaded on Me, as rows of pearls on a string.

—Bhagavad Gita

45

BEFORE the human heart can be tuned to vibrate to the Christ-note, the highest rate of vibration possible to human beings, it must be made capable of response to every note of sorrow and pain, every failure and shortcoming to which humanity is prone; for we cannot know the highest unless we also know the lowest, cannot experience heaven without experience of hell, cannot know the whole until we know every part.

The Christ is the keynote for humanity, and responds to every vibration and combination of vibrations within the human chord. Many people are most desirous of developing in themselves clairvoyance or clairaudience, which, to them, represent superhuman means of foretelling the future or looking into the past, of hearing words of prophecy and warning, or of becoming a wonder-worker and, consequently, a power in their particular circle. Those who think thus have no knowledge of reality. The true clairvoyant is one whose eyes are open to behold the beauty of God; and true clairaudience means that the inner ears can listen to every note sounded by the divine harmony. Those who have both powers fully developed also realize divine compassion, and so complete in themselves the threefold chord of love, harmony, and beauty. But before this chord can be sounded by a human being, the heart must be made so sensitive as to be able to vibrate with every note, and respond to every overtone and undertone in human life. One must know and understand the meaning of sorrow and sin, of shame and failure, of despair and bondage, and of physical, mental, and spiritual suffering. For it is only through realization of the inner meaning of these that the human heart can be tuned to respond to their opposites. The price of such realization is great indeed, but the reward is far greater, for upon one who has reached this stage on the spiritual path is conferred a title of the highest honor possible of human attainment, that of the Consoler, by which name such a person is from henceforth known to the fellowship of wisdom.

Blessed is the Consoler. Verily, the Consoler's sorrow shall turn to joy; for to the Consoler is revealed the secret of divine alchemy.

46

ONE of the most subtle temptations upon the spiritual path meets the disciples after they have traveled some distance and find certain powers beginning to unfold within themselves. Such things as inspirational speaking or writing, symbolic dreams, clairvoyant vision, healing power, and so on, attract a certain amount of attention and admiration, which, unless the disciples have become utterly indifferent to the opinion of others (a condition most difficult to attain), may be a very serious hindrance to their further development. It is not enough for them to say, even to themselves, that they are nothing but are only used as a channel, as this is a false humility and, in reality, in a subtle way, tends rather to glorify the personality and may become a far greater hindrance than open pride. Nothing that is said makes the least difference. It is the inner attitude alone that matters. When, in the innermost depths of the heart, there dwells the real spirit of humility, the atmosphere of such an one will speak for itself. There is no need for words.

The presence of one whose heart is attuned to God will radiate an atmosphere of harmony wherever that person goes, and even those who do not understand can feel and appreciate this.

It is deep calling unto deep: the call of God within the heart of the one heard by God in the heart of another, which, however deeply buried under error, can never fail to respond to the note of sincerity. Neither words nor actions can produce this response; nothing but a radiant atmosphere, the result of inner at-one-ment, can ever call it forth.

So long as words hold any meaning for the disciples, they will never know the inner reality .

> *He that hath received aught of Me, let him not boast of it; for in that hour shall the door be shut.*[1]
>
> —*Words Out of the Silence*

1 Dowland, Nargis Jessie, "Words Out of the Silence."

47

Be humble, if thou wouldst attain to wisdom;
be humbler still, when wisdom thou hast mastered.
—*H. P. Blavatsky,* The Voice of the Silence

TAKE heed, O traveler upon the path, when spiritual powers begin to unfold within you, for this is the time of your greatest danger. When worldly honor and fame have been renounced as worthless and empty, examine your heart lest the possession of spiritual powers means for you a greater honor, not in the eyes of worldly people, but in those of your companions upon the path. For verily, unless all such powers are, in true humility and prayer, held in trust for the use of humanity, the reaching of this stage of the path may be the disciple's undoing. "However holy a man may be, he will have to fight to the end, and chiefly against spiritual pride."[1]

Any power that may develop in one who is journeying to God is never for the use or glorification of one's own personality. One should consider oneself as simply the bearer of a gift of God to humanity, who must give an account of service to the master, from whom alone one receives the reward of further service. The gratitude and thanks of the recipient are due to the sender of the gift, not to the servant who delivers it. In the words of Lao Tzu, "The wise should be self-effacing, like snow beneath the sun." Self-effacement, or humility, the most illusive of the virtues, is of all things most difficult to attain. The one who thinks to have attained it is in reality very far away, for it cannot be found by seeking or by think-

1 Tauler, Johannes, *The Inner Way*. Sermon 8.

ing about it, and cannot be held while any thought of self remains.

So long as the disciple thinks, "I will be humble," "I will cultivate humility," the disciple will never understand; for it withers and dies where *I* lives. Only where *I* is forgotten in *Thou* can humility dwell.

O traveler in search of truth, deceive not yourself with words, nor cover the light of your soul with thoughts about your small self; for remember that the devil loves to clothe itself with a garb of spirituality, and false humility is one he very frequently dons.

Only *the proud in God* are the truly humble.

48

THE use of the word *mystic* suggests, to the minds of many people, wonder-working, hypnotism, or magic. And many will seek a mystic for the purpose of asking the mystic for some kind of magical power to help them in their business, or to obtain some particular object of their desire. There are, of course, some who claim to possess this power, and who practice their arts with more or less success. The real meaning, however, is very different. A mystic, really speaking, is a seer: one who sees God; not only a believer, but a seer of God, having purified the heart to behold the divine vision. "Blessed are the pure in heart, for they shall see God."[1] Yes! The mystic is also a wonder-worker, because a mystic has the faith that can remove mountains; but the only kind of magic used is the magic power of prayer, the greatest power there is. An alive faith in God, verily, enables the believer to perform miracles, for the believer knows the truth of the teaching that Jesus gave to his disciples: "For verily I say unto you, if ye have faith as a grain of mustard seed, ye shall say unto this mountain, 'Remove hence to yonder place,' and it shall remove: and nothing shall be impossible unto you."[2]

1 Matthew 5:8.
2 Matthew 17:20.

49

HOW difficult it is for human beings to find God, and yet if they could understand the relationship of God to humanity, all difficulties would melt away. God is the Sun, the One Light of the universe. The human soul is a ray of that light, which, when manifesting as a human being, finds itself gazing upon a world of changing shadows, and becoming interested in that illusion, identifies itself with it. So long as humans remain in this attitude, they cannot find God; for to do so, they must turn their backs to the shadows and face the light. They will then realize the true origin of the soul and cease to identify themselves with the material form.

Know the phenomenal forms are pitchers; with draughts of
the ideal.
Like a pitcher we are all being filled and emptied continually.
The draught is not derived from the pitcher, it comes from
another source;
Like the pitcher we are ignorant of the springs which
replenish it.[1]

—Jalal ad-Din Rumi

If one can keep the eyes of the soul steadily fixed upon the central sun, by the power of magnetic attraction the ray will be gradually up-drawn towards its center, until, losing the consciousness of separateness, one finds oneself in the presence of God.

It is almost impossible to give any idea to those who have not traveled the same path, of the feeling of absolute completeness

1 Jalal ad-Din Rumi, *Selected Poems from the Divani Shamsi Tabriz.*

experienced by one who is able to live in the constant realization of the presence of God, which is the goal of the mystic and the essence of the mystic's teaching.

Nothing can exist apart from God. Therefore, once a person has found God, every desire is satisfied. But the great difficulty lies in the realization of the truth of this teaching, for people think that to find God they must give up everything else. And that is true in one sense, because they must turn away from all that exists outside themselves in order to reach the kingdom of God within; for within and without are opposed to each other, and they cannot face both ways at the same time. They must endeavor to realize the truth underlying paradox, because it is the only way in which reality can be suggested. "He who would save his life must lose it"[2] cannot be too many times repeated, for whatever one gives up in order to seek one's God, one will find again in God, only in far greater measure, "The partial becomes complete; the empty, full; the worn out, new."[3] One will find the permanent reality of all things, instead of their changing shadows, which was all a person could ever know while living apart from God, Who alone is Reality.

While people try to stand separate and apart, with their backs to God, they are putting the shadow of themselves between their souls and the only light that can illumine their paths and give to them the supreme joy of the completed life.

In the light of the King's countenance is life.
—Proverbs 16:15

2 Matthew 16:25.
3 Tao Teh Ching.

50

Once you have given up your limited self willingly to the Unlimited, you will rejoice so much in that consciousness that you will not care to be small again.

—Inayat Khan

IF it were possible to describe in earthly language the true meaning of losing the self in God, it would give a very different impression to that of renunciation or sacrifice. "There is no such thing as sacrifice except in the imagination. There is opportunity to serve, and he who overlooks it robs himself."[1]

So long as humans desire the world and all it has to offer them, it is better that they should gratify those desires, as in any case, they cannot reach God, the goal of the disciple, while they are still desiring the life of the world; for no one can fly in the air and walk upon the earth at the same time.

When material pleasures and gratification cease to satisfy, when people become satiated with physical experiences, they will seek distraction in any kind of sensation or intoxication that will, as they term it, take them out of themselves. This is an expression in daily use, but the real meaning is seldom realized. Such a person does not know that the real reason of one's weariness of oneself is that the soul is seeking union with God and is athirst for a draught of the living water that gives eternal youth.

The part of a person that is desiring to be taken out is the real self of one who is longing for freedom to be in the presence of God, where there exists no burden of past, no fear of future, but an eternal today.

1 Mundy, Talbot, *OM: The Secret of Ahbor Valley.*

The soul is held in bondage by identifying itself with a false ego, which is in reality an illusion created by the mind, but from which it cannot escape until that which was created has been destroyed. "What the mind creates, the mind can destroy; but that which is born in the heart is eternal."[2]

Nothing but perfection can ever really satisfy any human soul, which can only be found by turning from self to God, Who alone is perfection.

2 Wallace, Mary Bruce, *Spiritual Reconstruction* (New York: Dodd, Mead and Company, 1919) 63.

51

THE pain and sorrow of the world, so difficult to reconcile with an all-loving and all-powerful God, may be understood by one who has mastered the law of rhythm.

Rhythm, or the inbreathing and outbreathing of God, is the means by which worlds come into being, and is inherent in every atom composing the universe, from angel to molecule. "The secret of birth and death is to be found in the mystery of breath."[1]

When God outbreathed, the universe was born. At God's inbreathing it will cease to be. "And the Lord God formed man of the dust of the ground, and breathed into his nostrils the breath of life; and man became a living soul."[2] Humanity, therefore, is subject to the law of the rhythm of breath. The soul, during its journey as a human being, needs the rhythm of day and night, light and darkness, joy and sorrow, union and separation, which are as necessary for its development as sun and shade are necessary for the development of the seeds of a flower. If they were always in the light of the sun, they could never come to maturity. The darkness of earth is necessary for them before flowers can be produced.

As the physical human body needs the dark of the mother's womb to become a living child, so the dual experience of light and darkness is necessary ere the Christ be born in the human heart. It is difficult for one to realize this necessity until one has eyes to see and ears to hear the things pertaining to the inner life. But when the heart has understanding, a

1 Inayat Khan, "Manifestation."

2 Genesis 2:7.

person will know that sorrow and pain are the birth pangs of the spirit, and that all things, whether pleasurable or painful, work together for good. For the whole world travails in pain until the Christ be born in humanity.

52

EVERY experience a human being contacts in daily life is full of significance, however apparently unimportant or trivial it may appear. In reality there is nothing that can be called trivial. Even those things that pass almost unnoticed are fraught with meaning for one whose spiritual sight is keen; and the result of any experience, no one can measure or see the end thereof. This is equally true on all planes of being. Every atom in the universe, from its highest spiritual expression to its densest form as physical matter, contains within itself life and motion, which are attributes of the Divine Being.

The infinitely great and the infinitesimally small are equally beyond comprehension by the human mind, for humanity has its dwelling place between these two extremes, unconscious of either. Only one who has attained absolute control of mind, and whose inner senses are awakened, can pierce the mysteries of the realm of spirit, where the two extremes of life meet and merge, the one into the other.

Whoever can solve the mystery of one will find the other open to view, for they are the beginning and the end in time of the One Eternal Being, beginningless and endless but which, by its own law of unalterable rhythm, is first the One, then the many, then again the One. And by this rhythmic law, the whole scale of vibrations, with its millions of overtones and undertones obeying the law of perpetual motion imposed upon them or, in other words, obeying the will of God, create, destroy, and recreate the manifold forms life uses for its expression in a physical world.

Whoever knows the mystery of vibrations indeed knows all things.[1]

—Inayat Khan

1 Inayat Khan, *The Bowl of Saki.*

53

KNOWLEDGE of truth and the realization of it are as far apart as earth is from heaven. Humanity may know everything there is to know and yet be far from the vision of God. Knowledge may be gained in various ways and can be imparted to those who are willing to give the necessary time for study and research. But to realize (i.e., make real in one's own life) is quite another thing, and belongs to the inner life. One second's vision of reality can teach more than a whole lifetime of study; but it is necessary for a seeker of truth to understand the law of paradox, for without some knowledge of truth, realization is not possible.

Many, misunderstanding this teaching, seek truth upon the path of knowledge and never progress further. Forgetting that it is a path that must be traveled to the end, they remain there, expecting truth to meet them, and fail to seek beyond it for the gate of illumination. Perhaps to call knowledge of truth *a path* is not altogether correct. Really speaking, it is the material from which one makes one's own path. Sometimes, of course, if it is well made, others may walk upon it. But unless the seekers understand that it is not the objective of the search but an open road leading to personal realization, seekers will block their own progress by building a solid wall across the way their feet should tread; and this, sooner or later, must be laboriously broken down by their own hands. For truth cannot be limited by facts; they are but stepping-stones formed of human understanding, which must be under the feet, and upon which one must stand fast to behold the vision of eternal verity. Without this aid, one will be in danger of sinking into the sand of incoherent and chaotic thought.

54

Take heed, therefore, how ye hear: for whosoever hath, to him shall be given; and whosoever hath not, from him shall be taken even that which he seemeth to have.

—Luke 8:18

IN these words of Jesus Christ is hidden a great mystery seldom understood by those who hear them. Indeed, they can only be fully comprehended by the awakened ones. "To him that hath shall be given." Hath what? And what shall be given? This is the promise difficult of comprehension, and to attempt an explanation almost entirely alters the inner meaning. Nevertheless, some few words may be given as a nucleus of thought. "Like attracts like" is a common saying in every language, because it contains a natural truth. All matter attracts atoms having the same rate of vibration. Even on the physical plane of existence, every element seeks union with itself. Water will seek and blend with water, and air with air; but in the subtle worlds, this is so in a degree impossible to explain. Thought attracts a like thought, and they become one with indescribably rapidity.

If this truth can be understood in its mystic sense, which in words can only be suggested, a vast and wonderful realm of the wisdom teaching is opened to the view. To the person who has within even one note in tune with the Christ-vibration, to that person will the Christ respond and live in full measure, pressed down and overflowing.[1] And as one can keep the rhythm of that vibration, so will one become filled with God.

1 See Luke 6:38.

But if the notes of one's life are out of tune, one cannot fill one's place in the divine harmony, and "even that which he seemeth to have" will be taken away. Although in the outer life one may to some extent deceive oneself, and even make others believe, that one is sounding a true note, in the inner life of the spirit there is no such possibility; for in the light of clear vision, all that *seemeth* will pass away.

55

ALL humanity is seeking happiness, but in order to be happy, one must be harmonious. This a person can only achieve by obeying the law of rhythm. Every situation in life has a beginning, a zenith, and an end; and unless humans understand and allow themselves to respond to this rhythmic vibration, or, as one terms it, obey the will of God, they cannot know happiness. When they refuse to go with the ebb and flow of life's tide, they are overwhelmed by its waves. Everything that life brings has a measure of time for its unfoldment and fulfillment, and after fulfillment must be loosed and let go. The secret of harmony lies in the knowledge of this truth.

All things must change; every moment the pattern alters, that life as a whole may become complete. Change is the law of life; nothing can remain without movement and live. When rhythm ceases, life ceases.

Of course, it is very natural that when one feels pleasure in any particular condition, one should try to make it permanent, because one is ignorant of the real nature of harmony. One does not know that by holding any experience longer than its appointed time, its measure becomes unbalanced and the rhythm lost, thus making it out of tune with one's environment and bringing sorrow and disappointment instead of happiness. A flower, if kept beyond the moment of its zenith, will begin to wither. If fruit is left upon the tree after the time of its perfection, it will decay.

The true harmonious life can only be realized by the recognition of the mystic teaching that what is held is lost, and whoever would gain life must lose it.

Disciples should hold all things lightly, ready to loose their hold when the hour strikes. When the inner meaning of this teaching is understood, they will never be fearful of losing; for as the spiritual vision unfolds, they will see and realize in themselves the mystery of surrender, which opens the door of the kingdom of God, and untold riches will lie at their feet.

56

THE beauty of thy garden, O Saki, intoxicates the soul of thy lover. Like the bee, the lover goes from flower to flower, gathering from each the living pollen.

The sweetness of honey is for the sustenance of thy worshiper, but its innermost essence remains in the worshiper's heart as pure joy.

57

BLESSED are those whose hearts are fixed; verily, they shall stand as a rock. When the waters of illusion surge around them, they shall not be moved. Neither shall they tremble, though all the waters of earth seek to dislodge them.

In the days of great tribulation they shall hold a light over the dark waters and guide My people into a place of refuge.

Verily, verily, they shall be blessed, for who so thus trusts can never fail.

58

THE blessed ones of God make themselves as a tower of light in the midst of life's ocean, to be a guide to those who are navigating its difficult seas. And while longing to live in the free air of heaven, they nevertheless build themselves firmly into earth, held down by rocks as hard as granite, in order that they may always be able to show the light over troubled waters in times of storm and darkness. Calmly they stand amid the storm and the whirlwind, through the waves of doubt that break upon them and the waters of tribulation that cover them. Verily, their lives are the living sacrifice offered afresh at each day's dawn, that humanity may be saved from shipwreck upon the rocks of illusion.

59

The veil between man and God is not earth or heaven, not the empyrean or the Throne. The veil is thy conceit and egoism;. when they are removed, thou hast arrived at God.

—Shaikh Abu Sa'id ibn Abi'l Khair

Wine From the Tavern

And lately, by the Tavern Door agape,
Came shining through the dusk an Angel shape
Bearing a vessel on his shoulder; and
He bid me taste of it; and 'twas the Grape.

The Grape that can with logic absolute
The two-and--seventy jarring sects confute:
The Sovereign Alchemist that in a trice
Life's leaden metal into gold transmute.

—Omar Khayyam

1

Grape juice does not turn to wine unless it ferment awhile in the jar.[1]

—Jalal ad-Din Rumi

ECSTASY is a mystical experience of the soul, sometimes called the sacrament of light, for in that moment of divine alchemy a transmutation takes place, and all the bodies of a human's being are temporarily raised to their original condition, thereby partaking of the soul's rapture.

It is this experience that produces the state that is called *vairagya;*[2] for once having known, even for a brief space of time, the condition of ecstasy, nothing that earth can offer could satisfy one thus conscious of exile.

The majority are content with such experience as pleasure and joy, which belong to the physical and emotional life of humanity. But ecstasy belongs to the soul life; and is reached by following the path trodden by the mystics of old, who in their writings frequently refer to this experience as a wine, for it produces in the human soul that divine intoxication in which the small self is completely forgotten.

The cupbearer is God, who intoxicates all creatures with the rapture of love. [3]

—Mahmood Shabistari

---

1 Jalal ad-Din Rumi, *Selected Poems from the Divani Shamsi Tabriz.*

2 Lit. "absence of passion."

3 Mahmood Shabistari, *The Mystic Rose Garden.*

2

Herein is my Father glorified, that ye bear much fruit; so shall ye be my disciples.

—John 15:8

I am the vine and ye are the branches, and my Father is the husbandman.

—John 15:1, 5

HE it is who prepares the winepress in which the fruit of the branches must be thrown and trodden underfoot, which by the divine alchemy of God is changed into the wine of Christ.

The treader of the winepress, knowing nothing of the process of transmutation, would naturally feel all was lost and that nothing remained but a mass of ruined fruit. But the Great Alchemist, who sees the end from the beginning, knows that fruit, if left upon the branches, will fall to the ground, rotten and useless.

Whosoever would drink the wine of life must yield the fruit of endeavor to the winepress of God. But once having tasted of that wine, there would remain no feeling of loss, nor desire for the fruit; for the essence of all fruit is contained therein.

The joy of a gathered blossom is but for a day. If that joy be renounced by those who can abide in faith the autumn harvest, they can gather fruit for their sustenance; but the one who is able still further to renounce and yield the fruit to be trodden in the press of life, awaiting in patience the time of its maturity, shall drink the sacramental wine. Verily, the one who drinks the wine of Christ shall never thirst.

3

"TAKE, eat, this is my body."[1] These words of Jesus Christ are, as are all his inspired utterances, capable of many interpretations, for they contain a profound truth that can be perceived according to the power of perception of the seer.

Food, when eaten or received into the physical body, ceases to be a substance separate and apart. It becomes one with the body it nourishes, part of and indistinguishable from it. Without such nourishment a physical body could not exist, and all the bodies used by the human soul must likewise be nourished and sustained, each by its own substance. As the material body needs material food, and the mental body mental food—knowledge of names and forms—so the spiritual body needs spiritual food: light.

Jesus the Christ said, "I am the light of the world,"[2] and "He that eateth me, even he shall live by me."[3] Whosoever therefore eats of the mystical body of Christ—his resurrection body of light—the Christ lives in them, brought to birth in this sacrament of light. "Ye in me, and I in you,"[4] is the beginning of the at-one-ment, for the spirit of all human beings is one spirit: the One manifesting as many under various names and forms—seeds of light buried in darkness, which, in order to become alive and active, must be fed and nourished by their own substance.

---

1 Mark 14.22.

2 John 8:12.

3 John 6:57.

4 John 14.20.

When all have been quickened, the many return again to and become one with, that from which they came forth.[5]

> *The consciousness of the One Whole is the flesh of Christ and the breath of love is his blood.*[6]
>
> — *Inayat Khan*

5 See Hebrews 11:15.

6 Inayat Khan, *The Gayan*.

4

Who shall say: "I have this day ascended another rung of the ladder which leadeth to Truth?" He only shall reach the summit who knows not when he is there.[1]

—*Sheikh Haji Ibrahim of Kerbela*

THE aspiration of every true seeker of God is service at the secret altar to tend the sanctuary light; but before such service is possible, one must, from oneself, provide the lamp and the oil for its burning.

A kindled heart is the only lamp that can illumine this altar and burn perpetually before its shrine, the Holy of Holies, where abides the presence of the living God.

But the cost? All that, as humankind, the human soul hopes, and feels, and knows. And the gain? A joy which cannot be spoken, and the exchange of illusion for reality, of the transient for the everlasting, of uncertainty for realization of the unchanging. Too high a teaching for those living the ordinary daily human life? Not if rightly understood, for it does not imply leaving life's duties, its pleasures, or its pains (for they are the life of human beings in the physical world, and without these the soul could not live as a human being), but to rise above them, not to be held by them, and to realize that *human* does not constitute the entire life of the soul.

When the desire for God-realization is entirely sincere, the intensity of desire will arouse the soul that is dreaming in a human being to behold the vision of imperishable things;

1 Sheikh Haji Ibrahim of Kerbela, *The Mystic Rose from the Garden of the King: A Fragment of the Vision of Sheikh Haji Ibrahim of Kerbela*, trans. Sir Fairfax L. Cartwright (1898).

and it is this awakening of the soul that lifts one above life's difficulties, not out of them, and gives strength to endure, not to evade them, but rather the courage to overcome, which is the greatest human achievement possible. "He that overcometh shall inherit all things; and I will be his God and he shall be My son."[2]

The way of the Yogi is that of asceticism and complete renunciation of earthly life, which is a different path to that of the mystic, for there are many paths leading to the goal. But in these teachings we are considering the possibility of a human soul knowing an inner life of the spirit while living the ordinary life in the world.

The realization that all material things, however difficult, and however important they may be for the moment, are in reality but illusions since they are transitory, gives the power to endure for a season; and also the understanding that beyond all illusion is the Eternal Reality, without which there could be no illusion, as there can be no shadow without its substance. If, therefore, your desire is sincere, and your soul athirst for the living God, and yet there is no consciousness of progress upon the path, be not dismayed; for "If with all your hearts ye truly seek Me, ye shall ever surely find Me."[3]

The servers at the secret altar are never conscious of their service, only of their desire for service. For while one can see oneself standing there in worship, however devout the worshiper, one is gazing at an illusion. But when one can see the faces of other servers, and utter thanks to God that they have reached the place where one fain would stand, in that moment (although but a moment of earth's counting) of entire self-forgetfulness, one will receive divine illumination, and realize, by the light of one's own burning heart, that in very truth, that worshiper is one with all people; and therefore, all faces one sees are one's own face, and all achievement

2 Revelations 21:7.

3 Mendelssohn, Felix, "Elijah."

one's own achievement and thanksgiving, for, verily, they all are one with the worshiper's own innermost self.

> *Losing himself outright, man finds himself*
> *in the Eternal Light.*[4]
>
> —*Hindustani Lyrics*

4 Inayat Khan and Jesse Duncan Westbrook, *Hindustani Lyrics Rendered from the Urdu* (London: the Sufi Publishing Society, 1919).

5

HUMAN beings are what they believe. Belief is an unshaken thought, and when faith is balanced by intelligence, a person may become a master of wisdom, although a fixed belief without intelligence many produce insanity—hence the great importance of a balanced life. It is, however, most necessary for pilgrims upon the spiritual path to understand the supreme importance of faith; for until they can do so, they will make very little progress toward the goal of their desire. It is not only faith in God, faith in a teacher, or faith in their fellow humans that they must hold, but the most essential of all: faith in themselves, which, if any would find God, must be unchangeable and unshakable. For unless one can believe in oneself, one cannot believe in any other being, either human or divine.

The mystery underlying this teaching is not easy to express in human language. It must be seen with the eyes of the soul to be comprehended; and when they are fully opened, the words of Jesus, "All things are possible to him that believeth,"[1] become illuminated. Some realization, however, can be attained by those who understand the creative faculty of the human mind. If, for instance, one begins to doubt the voice of intuition that speaks from the depth of one's own heart, and listens instead to the voice of reason, which can only judge those things that lie upon the surface of life but never what is hidden in the depths, then, by allowing thoughts to remain upon the surface, one creates an army of living entities,

1 Mark 9:23.

impressed with the purpose of instilling into their creator doubt of anything that cannot be examined by the light of cold reason, as it is called. One, therefore, questions one's ability to hear and interpret the voice that can only be heard when the mind is stilled and interpreted by the light of faith. Even after such an one has realized this teaching, and understands that reason alone can but give knowledge of the surface of life, and knows that intuition is the voice of wisdom, it is not always easy to listen; because the army of living thoughts one has created cannot be annihilated in a moment of time. They must accomplish the purpose imposed upon them by the will of their creator and, although now unable to take entire possession, will still endeavor, until their force is exhausted, to obsess their creator's mind whenever there is a thought of doubt in the heart. This is frequently a source of great suffering to an earnest seeker of God, for the greater the mind, the stronger are the thought forms it creates. They will, however, gradually fade away if not revivified by those of a like nature; hence the necessity of a right understanding of faith, for whenever a note is struck to which the forms of one's creation respond, not only are they revivified, but also others of like nature will gather around until one is enveloped in a cloud of uncertainty.

It may be likened to a number of steel filings that remain lifeless and inert until a magnet is held near them. Then all those within the magnetic field will become active and immediately rise up and surround it in a solid mass; but directly the magnet is removed, they again become lifeless. So if seekers can steadily hold belief in themselves, all the forms of doubt they have created will die for lack of sustenance. "For by faith ye stand."[2]

2 2 Corinthians 1:24.

6

LIFE can never be understood until it can be seen as a whole. It is this open vision that is sought by all seekers of truth, for to see for one moment the complete picture will give more knowledge than a lifetime of studying the separated parts. Much may be learned by a study of each isolated fact, of every factor in one's environment, and of the effect of every event upon one's own life and that of others. But although this will open a vast field of speculation and of interest, such a study will never disclose the plan, nor yield up the secret of the meaning of life. When people can see the whole as one vision, they will realize that everything in the universe, animate or inanimate; good or bad; earth, heaven and hell; from the dust of the Earth to the stars in their courses and all the hosts therein, has its own place in the great scheme, and not one could be left out. When they can hear life, not as a collection of single notes, which are meaningless, but as one great symphony, then will their ears be attuned to divine harmony. But while one note is unheard or considered unnecessary, or one thing, however small of seemingly insignificant, is left outside the range of their vision, they can never comprehend the grandeur of the unity in variety, or that perfection that is the Only Being.

7

God the Actor on the Stage of Life

If man is a garment worn by the soul, what is the soul—
wilt thou not say —of which I am the garment?[1]
—*Jalal ad-Din Rumi*

The world is but a stage, the stage of man,
On which the soul impersonates
Hero or slave, as best it can.

As actor in the play (which for the pastime of eternity
he doth himself contrive, enact, behold),
Sometime as king he struts across the boards,
Sometime as beggar, lowly and forlorn;
Again, as lover, priest or serf,
Differing only in the garment worn.

At fall of curtain—the same soul he was before the play began,
Save his experience and the skill
With which as player he did demonstrate the Author's will.

And if in drama, tragedy, or farce,
His lot it be to play as thief or rogue?
'Tis but another role
In the great Author's play,
And he, beneath it, still unsullied soul.

And when the robes of saint or sinner laid aside,
He seeks the place that is his own,

1 Jalal ad-Din Rumi, *Selected Poems from the Divani Shamsi Tabriz.*

After each part that he has played,
He lives the life that he himself has made.

The clothes he wore as servitor or king,
If they were beautiful, and he had kept them clean,
Another then may use them in the play,
Long after he has had his day.

The play the Author wrote will still
Be played, the robes designed for it can still be worn.
The wearers only will have changed,
Although to other players of the game
The actors still may seem the same.

But if the robes were badly used or marred,
Then on the rubbish heap they may be cast as waste;
Not to be lost—they will form parts of many things:
Small parts, perhaps of other robes—
Perchance of paper used by scribe or press,
But never can again as whole be actor's dress.

In time's great revolutions all must pass
Again into the void from which they came.
But then the play will cease, the Author rest a span,
Until another play He stages for the soul of man.

Yet still the truth in paradox lies hid,
The Author is Himself the players and the play,
The stage, the garments,
The failure and the skill;
And He the souls who demonstrate His will

8

Thy manifestation, O Blessed Lord,
neither Shining Ones nor Danavas comprehend.
— Bhagavad Gita

IF the whole manifest universe is an expression of the Only Being for the purpose of experience or self-realization, what or who is responsible for the suffering of humanity?

As nothing can exist apart from God, not even a devil, what is the human soul struggling against? Why the strife?

The strife is caused by illusion, or the shadow created by light; for light in manifestation becomes dual, thus creating its opposite. Therefore, humanity, in order to experience, is subject to the law of the pairs of opposites and can only regain reality through a right understanding of illusion. "This divine illusion of Mine, caused by the qualities, is hard to pierce; they who come to Me, they cross over this illusion."[1]

Divine life, the one living flame, manifests in the universe as manifold rays; and as a human being, the human soul is deluded by the illusion of separateness. By identifying itself with the physical and mental bodies by which it is enveloped, the soul gradually, according to the density of the form, loses consciousness of the oneness of its divine origin.

The God within is blinded by the solidification of spirit into matter, which, surrounding the soul as a shell, veils the vision of the God without.

Then of the Thee in Me who works behind
The veil, I lifted up my hands to find

1 Bhagavad Gita.

A lamp amid the darkness, and I heard
As from without—The Me within Thee blind![2]
—*Omar Khayyam*

The method taught in the ancient schools of Sufism, of regaining God-awareness, is that of *taubah* (turning), the reality of which lies in a continual turning from one's own nature. "May God make thee a seer of His, and remove thee from thyself."[3] The soul identifies itself with that which it beholds; hence, a seer of God attains God-identification.

As each ray of light in manifestation creates its own shadow, so each soul taking human form creates a false ego who claims a separate individuality.

A human soul who has attained balance can touch both the spiritual and material worlds and, while living the ordinary human life, can also hear and respond to the keynote of the soul, and knows the claim of separateness to be a false claim. But by identifying oneself with the false ego, one loses the rhythm of one's tuning and vibrates to discord. This is the cause of the unnecessary pain and suffering of humanity, but everything created is a creation in time and, therefore, has no existence apart from time.

God is the One Indestructible Reality, without beginning and without end.

Whose secret presence through creation's veins,
Running quicksilver-like – eludes your pains;
Taking all shapes from Mah to Mahi, and
They change and perish all—but He remains.[4]
—*Omar Khayyam*

Humanity is but a stage in the journey of the soul: "No other than a moving row of magic shadow-shapes that come and go."[5] The form perishes, the shadow passes, the great illu-

2 Omar Khayyam, *The Rubaiyat.*

3 Sharaf al-Din Maneri, *Letters from a Sufi Teacher.*

4 Omar Khayyam, *The Rubaiyat.*

5 Ibid.

sion ceases. That which remains is what was before the birth of time, and what will be when time has ceased to be. God remains, there is none beside. "I am the Lord, and there is none else. I form the light and create darkness; I make peace and create evil. I the Lord do all these things."[6]

> *I am the gambling of the cheat, and the splendor of splendid things I; and whatsoever is the seed of all beings, that am I; nor is there aught moving or unmoving, that may exist bereft of Me. . . .*
>
> *Having pervaded this whole universe with one fragment of Myself, I remain."*
>
> —*Bhagavad Gita*

6 Isaiah 45:6–7.

9

We are even as shadows, He is all who seek;
Lo, by Him is spoken every word we speak.[1]

—Jalal ad-Din Rumi

THE human soul cannot find God nor have any knowledge of God while imprisoned in its own mental creation. In other words, humans, as humans, are unable to realize God. When, either consciously or unconsciously, the desire for God has reached a certain pitch of intensity, the soul feels itself an exile and stranger in a far country, having lost the knowledge of its true origin and home. This condition is, for the soul, a veritable hell, and out of the depths it cries, "I will rise"; for in the darkness of despair when all seems lost, it begins to remember its real heritage and instinctively know that only by rising above the fetters of mind can it reach self-realization. Except in moments of ecstasy, when for a brief space the sense of *I-ness* is lost, it is difficult to rise from all that binds a human soul to earth. Great faith and a great courage are needed to cut the mental cords holding it captive, to rise alone into the unknown. But if the courage be great enough, the arising soul will see, while yet it is afar off, its own kinfolk coming to meet and welcome the soul to its own place; and will know itself no longer a prisoner of mind but a king's son, in the freedom of the Father's house. For in that moment of meeting, the at-one-ment of Father and son is realized. Every son is of the Father, and the son is in the Father, and the Father is in the son. They are one, and in this mystic conception it

1 Jalal ad-Din Rumi, *Selected Poems From the Divani Shamsi Tabriz.*

is the Father who was imprisoned and who arose, and who returned to the Father's own place. Earthly life, or the soul's journey as human being, is a condition created by the One Being from the Divine Self, in which God is, as it were, held in the illusion of God's own phenomena for the purpose of self-realization. The human being is a garment worn by the soul. "The uncovering of the soul is the discovery of God"[2]

> *I see Thee everywhere, unbounded form,*
> *Beginning, middle, end, nor source of Thee,*
> *Infinite Lord, infinite form, I find.*
> *Thou holdest all; then Thou Thyself art All.*
>
> —*Bhagavad Gita*

2 Inayat Khan, *The Gayan.*

10

God has said, "I am Truth." He has never said, "I am what you have been accustomed to believe."

—Pierre Abelard

WHEN seekers begin in earnest the search for God, they must necessarily experience a time of great bewilderment. For before they can recognize the reality that is God, they must understand and appraise the true value of the manifold forms of God made by creative human thought. To a sensitive soul this is sometimes a period of great mental agony, when all preconceived ideas lie in ruins about one's feet; and many times will one utter the cry, "Oh! That I knew where I might find God." But if the cry is sincere, the seeker should remember the promise of old: "'And ye shall seek Me and find Me when ye shall search for Me with all your heart. And I will be found of you,' saith the Lord."[1] Thus will be gained the courage to continue the search, for to a seeker of reality, bewilderment is an inevitable stage of the journey.

All images of God made by creative thought must, in time, be broken or they will bar the path of the pilgrim to the truth the pilgrim is seeking. But although every created form must eventually be disintegrated, nevertheless, all mental forms of God stand as milestones upon the road that one must travel, and can in no wise be dispensed with until their true value and meaning has been realized. Milestones are helpful and necessary at particular stages of travel, and without them a traveler may lose the way. But when one has reached the

1 Jeremiah 29:13–14.

journey's end, one has no further use for their guidance, although they remain necessary to those who are still journeying upon the same road. "A symbol is a resting for the mind, as it climbs the steps of reality." By slow and gradual steps the human mind is led through the real to the Real, through knowledge of created forms to the uncreated formless God, until the heart is awakened to seek in every form the impress of the Formless, and in every appearance, the shadow of the Real.

11

The rose in dread of autumn will flee from the garden.
His name will flee when it sees an attempt at speech.[1]
—Jalal ad-Din Rumi

THE sacred Name has ever been a great mystery that cannot be spoken; for naming means limitation to form, therefore, to name the unlimited is an impossibility. So in every age humans have invented some name by which they could call upon their God, some form that would satisfy their mental vision. Conceptions of the Supreme Being have been many and various, but every name that has been uttered in sincerity has reached the All-Pervading; and in every form selflessly worshiped, the Omnipresent has been adored. In every race, in every land, a different conception and different form of worship, a religion to suit the age and peoples, has been evolved. Always this has been, and always it will be, until humanity ceases to seek God in one form or under one name. How can the Nameless be named? Or the Unmanifest be conceived in form?

From the Formless, a diversity of form is generated. And from the Nameless arise innumerable names, for all forms are God's form and all names are God's name.

Behold, o Partha, forms of Me, a hundredfold, a thousandfold, various in kind, divine, various in colors and shapes.
—Bhagavad Gita

1 Jalal ad-Din Rumi, *Selected Poems from the Divani Shamsi Tabriz.*

12

The heart of man is the abode of God.
—Inayat Khan

AS a mere learning will never enable a person to know God, there is a certain amount of confusion of thought amongst those who aspire to read the path of seeking as to what extent the human mind can be used in the search. If knowledge of God cannot be attained by any mental process, then by what means can God be known? For if the reasoning faculty of mind is of no importance on this path, how can one know what one is seeking or recognize it when found, reason being an attribute of mind?

It is difficult to convey any solution of this question to one who has not realized the supreme mystery of humanity. A seer understands many things of which the seer cannot speak. To define a truth is to kill it, and the only motive for doing so is that a presentment of a dead fact will sometimes inspire a seeker to search for the living truth.

That which in a human being is striving to realize its origin and essence, is one's innermost being: the soul, or ray of divine light, which is one's life. All things else pertaining to humanity are instruments the soul uses for its expression and experience. The human soul, therefore, uses mind, with its reasoning power, for the purpose of the search; but although mind can seek, it cannot find. The mind can search and uncover everything that is obscure, it can sweep away and destroy every obstacle that stands as a barrier between a person and God; but to find and see that which the mind has uncovered, another faculty is needed: that of the heart. The mind seeks, the heart finds; for the mystery of God is hidden in itself.

The key to this problem lies in the fact that the heart cannot see until the mind has accomplished its work of preparation; but when it has done so, it is no longer a necessity in the search. The hands may uncover a treasure, but only the eyes can perceive it.

In the spiritual life of a human being, as in the physical, every faculty must be active, for all are necessary to the life of the whole. Not one must be allowed to remain inactive or unused, but each must be used for the purpose for which it was evolved. The mind cannot do the work of the heart; neither can the heart carry out the functions of the mind.

It is in the right understanding of unity that one will find the answer to one's questioning.

13

The mind is surface of the heart, and the heart is the depth of the mind.[1]

—Inayat Khan

TO attempt to define God is useless. Man (*manas* or mind) cannot conceive the greatness of God's majesty and glory. The utmost one can do is to wonder, to seek with all one's heart and endeavor to realize that most of the conceptions about God held by humans are human-made, imposed upon minds who are either averse to or incapable of any effort of individual thought, which must be developed by some method of concentration or meditation. The soul, buried under the dead thought of millions of brains, the accumulation of the ages, has become blinded; and until that burden is removed, the real search cannot begin. The God without can only be recognized by the God within, which, sleeping in the human heart, must be awakened from sleep by continual knocking upon the door. "Seek and ye shall find; knock and it shall be opened unto you."[2]

But as heart is the depth of mind, the unnecessary growths that have taken root upon the surface of heart, which is the mind, must be cleared away before the door can be reached and the soul freed to find the source of its being with seeing eyes. For the glory that is God, the perfection of all things, is far beyond the reach of mental vision or conception. Nevertheless, although it is the soul that finds, the mind must seek;

1 Inayat Khan, *The Art of Being and Becoming.*

2 Matthew 7:7–8.

and it is the seeking itself that will open the eyes of the soul, not knowledge; for if a person could be told what is God and what is human, and the mind were satisfied, that person would inevitably cease seeking; and consequently, the human soul would never find God. It is the restlessness of the mind refusing to be satisfied that impels one's whole being to seek and still to seek, to knock, and still to knock. For while one is searching, the mental vision is open; but if once a person were satisfied, believing there was nothing more to know, the eyes would close in sleep. "Taking all shapes from Mah to Mahi," God hides from humans, who by this means are kept awake and alert on every plane of their being, and lured ever onward in their search.

A moment guessed, then back behind the fold,
Immerst of darkness round the drama rolled,
Which for the pastime of eternity
He doth Himself contrive, enact, behold.[3]

—*Omar Khayyam*

An earnest seeker will continually get momentary flashes of vision, but before these can be translated into a satisfaction for the mind, the vision is gone and, at best, is as but a half-remembered dream. For under every living and breathing thing that surrounds humanity, the face of God is hidden; and it is the recognition of the light of God's countenance amid the shadows that gives such supreme joy to the seeker. "One flash of it within the tavern caught,"[4] that at any unheralded point of time may blaze in unimagined splendor across the path of a pilgrim of God, would give to the pilgrim the realization that not for one moment must the seeking cease, lest in that moment the light should flash some signal in the darkness, some letter of the alphabet of God.

A hair perhaps divides the false and true;
Yes; and a single alif were the clue—

3 Omar Khayyam, *The Rubaiyat.*
4 Ibid.

Could you but find it—to the treasure-house
And peradventure to the Master too![5]

—Omar Khayyam

5 Ibid.

14

ALL thought is not creative. Some thoughts are too feeble to be brought to birth, and many too chaotic to attain even the semblance of a form. It is the dominant thought that becomes the keynote of one's life and creates the nucleus of a person's condition and environment, which then, according to the rhythm of its tuning, attracts its own embodiment.

As the spider contains within itself the matter from which it evolves its environment (although invisible until materialized), so one's embodiment in this world and the next is made by oneself, from oneself, formed of one's own creative thought.

For this reason, masters of wisdom, who can see deeply into life, have always taught the importance of thought control. For unless humans can, in some measure, harness their thoughts and take their proper place as drivers, they will either be mastered by their own desires or else carried hither and thither without volition of their own.

Within every person is a kingdom, and there is nothing either of heaven, of earth, or of hell that is not contained therein. In this kingdom of mind, of which each person is ruler, one chooses a dwelling place by reason of the thoughts to which one gives birth. "Ye suffer from yourselves, none else compels. None other holds you that ye live and die, and whirl upon the wheel, and hug and kiss its spokes of agony."[1] "Within yourselves deliverance must be sought, each man his prison makes."[2]

1 Arnold, Edwin, *The Light of Asia.*

2 Ibid.

The way of escape trodden by the sages of old is to make God the dominant thought in the life: to think God until God is created; then to worship that creation until all thought of self is annihilated. The worshiper becomes one with the object of worship, when the life behind all form will be realized. No one can see God and live,[3] but upon the death of the self, when the lower surrenders to the higher, the form breaks. "For He is our peace Who hath made both one, and hath broken down the middle wall of partition between us."[4]

In that moment of mystical at-one-ment, about which no pen can write nor tongue speak, the living God awakes in the human heart, and the Christ Child is born. This is the second birth. The first birth is the birth of a human being, the second birth is the birth of God."[5]

Until human beings have themselves created a form that can be ensouled, God cannot manifest to them; although to find the living God, the created God must be broken. But fear not, O human.

> *If the form perishes, no matter, since the original is everlasting.*[6]
>
> *—Jalal ad-Din Rumi*

3 See Exodus 33:20.

4 Ephesians 2:14.

5 See John 3:6.

6 Jalal ad-Din Rumi, *Selected Poems From the Divani Shamsi Tabriz.*

15

THE lesson of the empty heart is a lesson that all pilgrims upon the spiritual path should strive to understand, although its inner teaching can never be known until self-realization has been reached.

The emptiness demanded of one who aspires to be used as a channel of divine force is no arbitrary demand but an absolute necessity; and the true meaning is detachment: detachment from the unreal. This does not mean that the heart becomes hard and cold, unable to respond to human love, but rather the exaltation of love by raising it to the highest point it is capable of attaining, until it touches and partakes of the quality of divine love. "Liberated from attachment, not egoistic, endued with firmness and confidence, unchanged by success or failure, that actor is called pure."[1]

When, in one who has thus prepared, this purification is fulfilled; self will be entirely obliterated. And the heart, which is the shrine of God, becomes empty of all save God, detached from anything that could rebuild the self, or false ego. Unless this stage has been reached, the human heart cannot be used to transmit the pure message of God; for if the channel be not empty of all that is foreign to truth, its white purity is colored by the thoughts and desires emanating from the false ego. "'For My thoughts are not your thoughts, neither are your ways My ways', saith the Lord."[2] Therefore, a deliverer of God's message must be free from human ways and from human thoughts.

1 Bhagavad Gita.
2 Isaiah 55:8.

Is it surprising that in all ages the messenger, in whom self has been silenced that God may speak, has been misunderstood, or that the messenger's earthly life has been a crucifixion, when the words the messenger utters and the thoughts to which the messenger gives birth are exactly the opposite to the ways and thoughts of those amongst whom the messenger dwells, uncomprehended by those who attempt to judge words and teachings by the limited standard of human intelligence?

Unless one will endeavor to learn the wisdom language used by all the illuminated souls who have brought God's message to the world, one will never understand the messenger.

16

THOSE who aspire to lighten the darkness of ignorance must first kindle a fire within their own hearts. For the flame arising from a burning heart is the only light that can guide the feet into the way of peace.

As there is no fire without destruction of form, so the flame of love demands sacrifice. The fire lighted in the human heart must be continually fed with the nonessentials of life and the qualities pertaining to the false ego, so that reality, or the essence of all things, may be set free to ascend as light. It is this conception that lies behind the idea of burnt offering and sacrificial fires; a spiritual trust interpreted physically, as all truth is interpreted by those who are not yet come to the full human stature. Spiritual realities expressed in symbols are capable of many interpretations, according to the evolution of insight of the seer. But the mystic truth underlying burnt offerings is the sacrifice of the lower to the higher.

As humans evolve, their eyes gradually open to the realization that only by such a burning can the light of guidance be produced, which will light one's own path and also that of others; that to possess, one must sacrifice; to live, one must die, that from the ashes of the dead self one may rise, as the phoenix arises—a newborn soul.

When human beings are born again they enter the path leading to divine illumination, and the illuminated souls become as a burning torch in the darkness. These great ones, although unconscious of their service to humanity—as light is ever unconscious of itself—by reason of their own illumination and the power of its light, act as guides to those who are striving to find a way through the dark clouds of mental obscurity to the dawn of spiritual light.

Verily, they are blessed who understand the mystery of the burning heart.

17

Verily I say unto you, whosoever shall not receive the kingdom of God as a little child, shall in no wise enter therein.
—Luke 10:17

ONE must become as a little child before one can be a pupil of God and learn those things that are hidden from the wise and prudent, and revealed unto babes.

Whosoever would watch the unveiling of the mysteries, when all that is hidden shall be revealed,[1] must be stirred by the spirit of wonder; for it is this spirit that can open the heart to behold the things that eyes may not see, nor the human mind conceive.

The kingdom of heaven is in the human heart, and "Heaven lies about us in our infancy,"[2] because to a child all things are new and wonderful; and until "shades of the prison house begin to close about him,"[3] the child lives in a state of belief and expectancy that makes all things possible. Humans, therefore, in order to regain the freedom they have lost, must rediscover the state of wonderment, for they are still in bondage until all things become new to them. It has been said that at every moment one must be born, or at each moment one dies a little.

To win the right of entry into Wonderland is to possess the secret of eternal youth, for time has not power to age the heart that is open to wonder. It is the greatest gift of God to

1 See Mark 4:22.

2 Wordsworth, William, "Ode on Intimations of Immortality," from *Recollections of Early Childhood*. II 67–68.

3 Ibid.

humanity, annihilating time and space, and giving the freedom of both worlds. *Wonder* is the word of power, making all things new: the golden key that will unlock the mystery of life that all are seeking.

> *Let not him that seeketh cease from his search until he find; and when he finds, he shall wonder; wondering he shall reach the kingdom; and when he reaches the kingdom he shall have rest.*[4]
>
> —*Jesus*

4 *New Sayings of Jesus* (Oxford, 1904), discovered 1897.

18

ANY thought conceived in the human mind must necessarily be less than the person, as the creation is less than the creator. Whatever ideal of God one holds is a created thought and, therefore, cannot be the God of reality, Who, having created humanity in God's Own image, is greater than and beyond conception by God's creation. When anyone holds an ideal of the Supreme Being, so great that it touches perfection, it is because one has focused the heart upon the God within, thus becoming a reflection of the One Light, "Which lighteth every man who cometh into the world."[1]

No one can see God and live.[2] When Jesus said, "If ye have seen me, ye have seen the Father also,"[3] it was by reason of God-identification: having died to self he lived as God. The soul must know its true origin and identify itself with the One Light, of which it is a ray, before the reality that is God can be realized. Only by becoming one with God can a human being behold God; by dying to the separated individual life, can a human live in the whole universal life. It is the mystic journey of the soul, the turning and the coming from self to God.

God is love. Human beings, therefore, made in the image of God must ever seek an object of worship, for the need of worship is innate in every soul, however deeply it may be buried. But being limited in a world of name and form, humanity cannot comprehend the unlimited. Hence, it is only

1 John 1:9.

2 See Exodus 33:20.

3 See John 14:9 and 8:19.

by creating and destroying ideal after ideal of a God Whom they can worship, that they reached God-identification.

> *As God is all and all is God, he who is absorbed in the divine essence becomes identical with it.*[4]
>
> —*Jalal ad-Din Rumi*

4 Jalal ad-Din Rumi, *Selected Poems from the Divani Shamsi Tabriz.*

19

ONE reaches perfection when, on every plane of one's being, the pairs of opposites are completely balanced. The trinity of life is love, harmony, and beauty. The balance of love is lover and beloved; the balance of harmony is silence and sound; the balance of beauty is light and shadow. When these are in equilibrium and the divine fire of the living God touches a person's life, one's whole being is transmuted from a solid condition, bound by time and space, to that of freedom. And as ice, when melted by heat, will ascend in the form of vapor, becoming one with the atmosphere that is its source, so humanity, when freed from bondage, will arise to seek the source of its being and become one with it.

20

EACH person creates their own evil and good, their heaven and their hell. The environment in which they live is their own creation, the embodiment of their thoughts and desires. Those who would change their environment, let them change their desires; then their thoughts will take different form, and their environment gradually shape itself according to their desire.

21

GOD, the center or positive force, creates the negative from God's own Self, thus making capacity—i.e. *akasha*—and worlds are born.

A creation must be negative to its creator. As Eve was negative to Adam, distinct from him and yet being made from Adam, she could have no existence apart from him. So the universe is not God, and yet is not "not God"; emanating from God, it is therefore of God.

Spirit-matter, or substance, of which is formed all created things, is the breath of God. God outbreathes, and a world takes birth. At God's inbreathing, it ceases to be. Being created, it contains within itself, as must all creations, the hour of its cessation as a concrete form, and returns to its original condition of pure spirit. In the act of outbreathing, breath becomes dual; and from kemal (perfection) arise jelal and jemal (positive and negative). Thus is formed the substance of a world of duality, which in its essence is pure spirit, but in manifestation becomes solid.

As the breath is exhaled, it gradually becomes more and more substantial until it entirely solidifies and, in this condition, is known as substance or matter.

> *Outward form is an illusion, which dissolves at the word of God.*[1]
>
> — *Jalal ad-Din Rumi*

> *Matter is a state of spirit.*[2] — *Inayat Khan*

1 Jalal ad-Din Rumi, *Selected Poems from the Divani Shamsi Tabriz.*

2 Inayat Khan, *The Gayan.*

22

THE majority of those who profess a desire to know truth cannot recognize reality when they are face to face with it.

The real is hidden under so many veils that it is necessary to know these before one can find what they cover, which is a process very few care to undertake, for the time and trouble needed is well-nigh endless. Nevertheless, if the sight of the seeker is single and unwaveringly fixed upon the goal, the seeker will never be deceived by a counterfeit of truth, however cleverly it may be presented. Neither will one whose spiritual eyes are open fail to discover reality, whatever the garb under which it is hidden.

23

THE true knowledge of God is hidden in humanity. And when the window of the heart, through which a human soul views life in the world, is darkened from without by the hand of God, it is in order that it may become as a mirror in which human beings can see themselves; for when it is entirely covered upon the outer side, it reflects the real or inner self, the Father in heaven. But when there is no such darkening, then only those things that the mind creates can be seen.

The darkening is in response to the desire of the soul for the light of truth. Such a covering obscures all images passing upon the outer side, thus making the human heart like unto a mirror whose reflecting surface, facing inward, or Godward, can reflect nothing but God. Here the analogy breaks down, because the heart is a living mirror; and when it has been made capable of reflecting God in the inner life, it can, at the same time, reflect God upon the outer life. And the light of this reflection becomes a powerful ray, which, when turned upon the transitory things of earth, has the effect of making them invisible, so that the heart in which God is mirrored sees only God, either in the inner or the outer life.

Give to my heart, O God, the searchlight of the open vision, that when it falls upon Thy beauty all else may become shadow.

24

NO person is compelled by any outside compulsion to search for truth. One who is content with truth's counterfeits will remain satisfied until the demand of the soul for the environment it has lost is too insistent to be denied. But when once the human mind has listened to the voice of the soul and felt the divine urge for God, then nothing can hold one back from pursuit of reality.

It is often a great bewilderment to many seekers of God why, upon the path of seeking, they should meet with every kind of delusion; and many times they feel disheartened that they, who seek only beauty, are brought face to face with ugliness, unreality and disappointment. It is at this stage of the journey that doubt assails them—doubt sometimes even of the existence of God, for they argue: "If God exists, how should God allow such things to cover the eyes of those who are striving to turn from darkness to seek the light of God 's presence?"

It may be of some help to those who cannot yet see beyond the doubt that envelopes them, if they will strive to realize the method by which a soul seeking truth may find it. While human beings are living in a world of duality, they cannot have knowledge of anything unless they also know its opposite, otherwise life would be meaningless. The one who would know God, the One Reality Who is love, light and truth, must also realize evil, darkness and unreality. And the greater the soul's demand for reality, the greater will become the power of recognizing the unreal. Thus this stage upon the path of a pilgrim of God is necessarily one of bewilderment, because humans must face with open vision, and become identified with, pain, suffering and the darkness of doubt in order to realize, and so avoid, the illusion of identification with the unreal. When seekers are surrounded on every side by clouds of illusion hiding from the vision of God, they will not feel despair if they have faith to believe and can hold fast to the underlying truth that reality is behind all illusion, as light creates its own shadow, which, without light, could have no existence.

Faith will then become a torch and will guide the seeker's feet through the places of bewilderment to a sure and certain knowledge of the presence of the living God, leading to the ineffable joy, about which no word can be spoken, of God-identification.

25

God says, 'Who gropes towards Me an inch through
doubting dim,
In blazing light do I approach a league towards him.

— *Anonymous*

THE mystic is sometimes thought of as a dreamer or visionary, raised so far above the ordinary daily human life as to be incapable of understanding its many difficulties. Hence the mystic path holds little attraction for a person of the world, but this is not a true conception.

A mystic or seer is one who has attained the power to see the mystery, or inner meaning, of all things, whether of so-called good or bad, spiritual or material; for all are but covers of the one truth. In other words, a mystic is a knower of the veils. And far from not understanding human life in the physical world, one could not be a real mystic unless one had first realized in oneself, and then risen above, every phase of human life lived in a world of humanity. Very few are able to reach this high stage, only the great souls who have conquered themselves. But it is open to all to take the first steps, and whosoever takes one step upon the mystic path of return to God, God will take two to meet them.

26

ALL great teachers and mystics of the past have taught, either orally or in their writings, that to find reality it is necessary to pass through illusion.

It is difficult to realize the value of this teaching, but those who desire to tread the path of return must endeavor to gain some understanding of its inner significance.

No one is compelled to return to God upon the path trodden by the mystics of old. There are many others, and each soul must choose the one to which that soul is attuned; for all paths, in the end, lead to the one way. But having chosen the swift path of mysticism, a seeker will sooner or later be faced with the great problem of illusion.

One of the most difficult stages is when one realizes that all one's world, and everything it contains of pleasure and pain, is but a dream before the soul; and all that one had thought of as solid and lasting is crumbling about one's feet, having no foundation. This will lead the earnest seeker to the path of unknowing, where the seeker will understand the necessity of realizing the nature of illusion. For without such realization, it would remain for the seeker, as it is for most dwellers in the material world, the only reality one could know.

A high courage, steady perseverance and great power of will are needed to tread the path of unknowing in safety. For this reason the guidance of one who has knowledge of the path should be sought, as the guide can see how far into the valley of bewilderment it is safe for the traveler to adventure.

The uncovering of the veils brings a great bewilderment. And if undertaken for the purpose of gaining knowledge and power; to gratify curiosity; or even to enable one to, as one terms it, *work for God*, (as if all work, however apparently insignificant, were not God's work); or for any other purpose whatsoever other than an intense desire to behold a vision of truth in which self and all that pertains to it can be entirely forgotten, the seeker will fall by the wayside.

Very gradual must be the journey. And before each uplifting of the seventy thousand veils that cover truth, the heart of the seeker must be purified of selfish motive; for only the pure in heart can see God.

This may appear to some a quite impossible task for any to undertake, but it depends upon one's point of view. If it is seen as a task meaning a forcible breaking away from all one holds dear, from one's duties and desires, it would naturally appear unending. But if the seeker can, even for one moment, daily turn the heart to the contemplation of the beauty of God, in that moment and for that space of time, everything is forgotten in wonder; for the seeker has turned from death to life, where time and the things of time are nonexistent.

"The gift of God is eternal life"[1] that humans may attain by seeking. "Continue thy seeking until the seeking unveils itself and destroys thyself in thee. Henceforth the disciple has nothing to do; the seeking will itself lead him on."[2]

1 Romans 6:23.

2 Sharaf al-Din Maneri, *Letters from a Sufi Teacher*.

27

THE difficulties and tests that await a pilgrim upon the path of return must be judged from a different viewpoint from that of the ordinary person, although the difficulties encountered by each may be the same. But to one who has set a foot upon this path, life and everything it means must be regarded from a different standard to that of one who has not yet done so.

The result of every test that life brings is not the essential thing. Whether a person succeeds or fails is of the greatest importance to that person as a human being. This fact must never be lost sight of; but in the life of one who is seeking to attain the condition of *hu-man*,[1] success and failure belongs to the life of illusion, as both will pass.

That which matters to the treader of the path is the evolution of certain qualities that are brought to birth by the result of one's action and reaction to the conditions of one's environment.

The possibility to evolve such qualities is latent in all. But in order that they may become alive, or active, one must meet every kind of test and difficulty; and success does not always mean success, or failure mean failure. What should be remembered is that it is the qualities themselves that matter, not their effect upon a person; for, as a stage in the soul's life, the human being passes.

---

1 *Hu-man* or divine man. The word *Hu* is said to be the most ancient term for God.

When God-identification is attained, all these qualities become the seeker's servants and obey the seeker's will until the end of time; for this is the true heritage of the human soul.

28

THOSE who fail to conform to the orthodox teaching of their time are always looked upon with suspicion by the majority. Jesus was called a blasphemer because he dared to claim his divine sonship. The people could not interpret the mystery underlying his utterance nor understand the symbolism of the mystic union of Father and Son. Few, even of those nearest to him, comprehended his message to them after his resurrection: "Go to my brethren and say unto them, I ascend unto my Father and your Father, and to my God and your God."[1] Even today, after two thousand years have passed, it is equally misunderstood. The religious Christian will accept Jesus as the Son of God but believes him to be the only son. Such an one will also pray to "Our Father" but would consider it blasphemy to think Fatherhood implies sonship, which is a curious anomaly.

From the beginning of time, God has spoken to humanity through God's son. From the foundation of the world, all great souls who have reached the stage of at-one-ment with their Father in heaven are called *Sons of God*. "For as many as are led by the spirit of God, they are the Sons of God."[2] and are used as God's instruments and messengers; for God speaks to unawakened human beings through human lips.

The beginning of this divine relationship is the mystical birth of Christ in the human heart: the second birth that, unless one experiences it, one cannot inherit the kingdom of God. "But if the spirit of Him that raised up Jesus from the

1 John 20:17.

2 Romans 8:15.

dead dwell in you, He that raised up Christ from the dead shall also quicken your mortal bodies by His spirit that dwelleth in you."[3]

Those who once have received the adoption of *son*, can nevermore separate themselves from the Father's love, nor feel as a stranger in the Father's house. "The servant abideth not in the house forever, but the son abideth ever. If the son, therefore, shall make you free, ye shall be free indeed."[4]

In order to attain to sonship, the human soul must pass from the condition of Ishmael—the state of bond slave—by fighting to the death for freedom. "For the son of the bondwoman shall not be heir with the son of the free woman."[5] One must, like the phoenix, arise a new being from the ashes of the dead self, for only after the death and burial of the old self can resurrection be experienced as a living truth. Thus passing through death into life, one will reach realization of the Fatherhood of God and of one's own royal birthright. No more as a bondman compelled unwillingly to labor, but by voluntary surrender of the self to the Self, one will, from henceforth, work as a son about the Father's business. "Wherefore thou art no more a servant, but a son; and if a son, then an heir of God through Christ."[6]

The whole teaching of the relationship of humanity to God is far too mystical and wonderful to be explained by any human thought or speech; neither can it be comprehended in its entirety by any human being. Nevertheless, meditation upon the idea will reveal, to those who are in some measure prepared to receive it, a vision, if albeit but a fleeting one, of the divine Fatherhood. "Stand fast, therefore, in the liberty wherewith Christ hath made us free, and be not entangled again with the yoke of bondage."[7]

3 Romans 8:11.

4 John 8:35–36.

5 Galatians 4:30.

6 Galatians 4:7.

7 Galatians 5:1.

29

Our celestial spirit is free to eternity,
Tho' for a short while we have the shape and figure of man.[1]
—*Jalal ad-Din Rumi*

TO attempt in words an interpretations of *nirvana* is useless, for those whose spiritual eyes are opened know and, therefore, need no explanation; and by the majority, who make of every living truth a dead fact, its real meaning will always be misunderstood.

The conception that human beings should ever lose their individuality is so unacceptable to the ordinary mind that it cannot imagine such a thing to be possible; and generally, what is beyond human understanding, a human being does not wish to believe. The teaching embodied in the ancient mystic philosophy, that at the end of manifestation all beings are absorbed into the One from Whom they came forth and no individuality remains, is inconceivable and unattractive to such thinkers; so much so, that it has been responsible for a school of thought that teaches the imperishable individuality of the person. In reality, both these teachings are right from one point of view. "Children, not sages, speak of the *Sankhya* and the Yoga as different; he seeth who seeth that the Sankhya and the Yoga are one."[2] The difficulty lies in human ignorance of the true conception of humanity. A human soul, as human, cannot retain an individuality, for humanity is an expression or manifestation of the soul, for a limited

---

1 Jalal ad-Din Rumi, *Selected Poems from the Divani Shamsi Tabriz.*

2 Bhagavad Gita. Sankhya and Yoga are two schools of Hindu philosophy.

time and for a special purpose. When the hour strikes and the purpose is accomplished, the soul travels far beyond human limitation.

Ice cannot retain its individuality as ice. Water becomes ice for a time and for a purpose but can never lose its identification with water. When the "dewdrop slips into the shining seas,"[3] it is one with the consciousness of the ocean and indistinguishable from it. Although from the ocean, innumerable dewdrops may arise and fall, they are dewdrops only during the time of separation from their source. When they return again to that from which they went forth, their dewdrop individuality is absorbed. But there is no loss by such a merging; the real loss is during the limitation as a separate drop.

People are sometimes repelled by the teaching of annihilation, but this is only while they are ignorant of its real meaning. It is true that the path ends in annihilation, but annihilation of what? Not of life, not of being, not of consciousness; all these are increased a thousandfold, for the perfection of all is reached; but annihilation of the separated self, which the mystic voluntarily seeks because the mystic has been face to face with it and has seen with the eye of the spirit and, therefore, understands its true worth and use.

The mystery of self must be uncovered by each one with one's own hand, ere the light that is behind all illusion will show the inner truth of one's own being.

> *"The self of matter and the Self of spirit can never meet. One of the twain must disappear; there is no room for both."* [4]
>
> —*H.P. Blavatsky*

Those who, resenting the mystic's ideal of losing the small self in the Divine Self, desire to retain their own individuality after the death of the body, need have no fear: they will certainly see the fulfillment of their desire so long as they desire

3 Arnold, Edwin, *The Light of Asia.*

4 Blavatsky, Helena Petrovna, *The Voice of Silence.*

it. But sooner or later that desire will change, for the burden of themselves will become more than they can bear. Who would have courage to face, with open vision, an eternal life shut in with one's own individuality, never to be free from the prison house of memories, from one's own ideas, from the shadow of one's life's mistakes and shortcomings?

The greatest joy it is possible for a human being to experience is found not in possession, but in surrender. For in the supreme act of self-giving, one becomes no longer a bondslave but a free human being.

So long as people hold that which they cannot lay down, they remain with their possession, held by it as securely as prisoners are held by the chains with which they are bound. But in ignorance of this truth, people bind themselves ever more securely with the fetters of false identification, crying out in their bondage, "Who will deliver me from the body of this death?"; blaming God or fate or their fellow humans for the failure to release themselves. There is, however, no power on earth, in heaven, nor in hell which can release one from oneself other than the surrender of one's own thoughts about oneself. So long as a person thinks, "I am a separate individual apart from and independent of either God or my fellow humans," that person will remain a prisoner of self. Alas, humans are blinded by the great shadow of their own importance. If they could but realize the soul's true origin and destiny as part of a mighty whole, and by surrender partake of the consciousness of this whole, instead of being aware only of the infinitesimal part, they would find not only freedom, but the kingdom and the power and the glory.

The Notebook

Foreword

NARGIS Dowland's notebook was written between 1919 and 1927 according to dates within the manuscript. In the summer of 1930, she gave the notebook to Sirdar van Tuyll,[1] another mureed of Hazrat Inayat Khan. The notebook contains inspired sayings and passages written by Nargis, some accounts of her experiences with her murshid, Inayat Khan, and some quotations from Inayat Khan himself, which were taken down verbally by Nargis. Nargis told Sirdar that some of the sayings not attributed to Inayat Khan "are not Murshid's exact words, but that she guarantees that the sense is Murshid's."[2] Although sections of the notebook were used as source material by Nargis when she wrote her books and essays, the notebook is presented here in it's known entirety.

1 "Sirdar" was the Sufi name of Hubertus Paulus baron van Tuyll van Serooskerken.

2 Notes on the cover of *Miss Dowland's Notebook.*

1

INITIATION is a trust; it is a gift, a relationship formed between the pupil and the teacher. But knowledge cannot be given any more than the voice producer can produce a voice when there is none to produce. Every soul that is spiritually evolved has the necessity for initiation.

One thing is true: that Murshid[1] cannot give the knowledge, but he can kindle the light if the oil is there.

1 In this notebook, *Murshid* refers to Hazrat Inayat Khan, Nargis Dowland's own murshid, or Sufi teacher and guide.

2

SYMBOLISM of refusal of the wise virgins to give their oil to the foolish:

Every soul must have its own oil. They could not give their oil. It is not a substance that you can give to another. The teacher, however great, can never give knowledge to the pupils. The pupils must create their own knowledge. The teacher can help to kindle the light in the lamp. That is why God is called *Khudda* by the Persians: because God is the One Who comes by God's own Self.

3

ASCETICISM has always been practiced by the seekers after truth. At some period of evolution, asceticism is done by everyone; it is a necessity of the soul.

Willpower is the keynote of mastery, and asceticism is the development of willpower.

Anything forced from without is of no use. Asceticism was not encouraged by Mohammad, but the Prophet had his days of asceticism. Asceticism in catholicity had gone to great extremes, and it was necessary to bring about a balance. Everything is suited for a certain period, and the same thing is not suited for another period.

Murshid told that he was born with a tendency towards asceticism. As a child he had a great love for sweets and nice things, but when he was very young, someone told him that the brave must take bitter and sweet alike, and whatever comes.

Once Murshid was ill, and pills and bitter powders would be given to him. As soon as Murshid heard this, he said to himself that he would be brave and take them. And from that time, his parents told him, he never hesitated to take anything that was offered to him without even making a face.

4

ONCE when Murshid was standing with Miss Dowland[1] before a dilapidated old church, Miss Dowland said to him, "Oh, Murshid, shouldn't we buy this and rebuild it for the Sufis?" Murshid answered, "Never, never, never will Murshid found a church." A week later, Murshid dictated to her, at her flat in Southampton, the "Service of the Universal Worship." It was then and there that the Church of All came into existence.

Murshid told her that all the attendants of the service should sit on the floor. "Very well, Murshid," she answered, "but then nobody will come." After this, they were allowed to sit on chairs.

1 In her notebook, Nargis Dowland writes of herself in the third person.

5

MURSHID, going to give a lecture, said to Miss Dowland on entering the hall. "What is the my subject for tonight?" She answered, "The power of the word." Murshid, mounting the platform, announced, "I speak tonight on the power of silence."

In Switzerland it once happened to Sirdar too, that Murshid, before going to give a lecture, asked, "What is my subject for tonight?" Sirdar answered, "The word that was lost," whereupon Murshid turn round to Sirdar, saying "There was never a word lost." Then he mounted the platform and gave a beautiful lecture on "The word that was lost."

6

ONCE, when staying with Miss Dowland at her hotel,[1] Murshid fell ill. The next morning Miss Dowland asked him if he had slept well. Murshid answered, "It has been a terrible time; my army refused to obey me."

1 Nargis Dowland was the manager of the Polygon House Hotel in Southampton, England.

7

MISS Dowland told that a young man asked Murshid, "Will you take me as your pupil?" Murshid asked him, "Have you faith?" "I have faith in you, sir." Whereupon Murshid said, "That is of no use to me. Have you faith in yourself?"

8

MURSHID used to say to Miss Dowland, "I impart in you my light, my life, my strength, my power, my joy, and my peace."

As her busy life did not allow her much time for meditation, this was the way in which Murshid helped and trained her: asking her to remember and repeat these words every time before going to bed. Murshid also said to her, "Be content to know nothing, to be nothing. Just give me your service."

9

MISS Dowland told, "Once I had a concert at the Polygon Hotel and Murshid sang, with the vina, different songs. I never saw Murshid alone in the hotel, and I wanted to see him alone. I took a taxi and sought in the New Forest for a place. At last I found a small hotel, and by the side of it was a little annex. There were two sitting rooms and a very large kitchen, three bedrooms and a room with a bath in it. I took that on May 31st till June 3rd, 1919. It was called "New Forest Inn." It was in Emery Down. After the concert we just got into a taxi, Murshid, Murshida Green and myself, and we drove there—on a Saturday, I think.

While we were there, Murshid took the vina in the middle of the forest. We sat on a rug and we were quite alone. We sat for hours in the morning and spoke. And Murshid sang, and we did not know where we were. It was like Omar Khayyam say, "Tomorrow? Why tomorrow I may be myself, with yesterday's seven thousand years."[1]

We had to come to Southampton for a lecture on Sunday. On the Monday we went into the forest. Murshid said, "Now we will take one day out of eternity." A telegram came that Mamuli[2] was born. We went back by taxi.

1 Omar Khayyam, *The Rubaiyat*.

2 Khairunissa Inayat Khan, Murshid's youngest child.

10

MISS Dowland once dreamed that she saw Murshid sitting on one of the bridges across the Thames on a bench, with at every side, a woman of the street, tired and asleep, resting against him. She wondered why Murshid remained sitting like that. And she asked Murshid later on for an explanation.

Murshid gave the following explanation: "In my physical body I am limited as an ordinary man. How could I help those women, who were asleep on every plane of their being, except by thought? They could not even see me, nor would they have understood if they had. My work here is to find those who are already awake on the inner planes and to touch their souls that they may also awaken on this to see through the veil of physical matter, and thus prepare a few sowers for the field of God, who may be trusted to sow the living seed, the fruit of which shall be for the healing of nations, the bread of life given without money and without price to all who ask. And in those days there shall be no starving bodies, for they are the result of starving souls. Labor and toil without ceasing, to prepare the field for the sowing. And remember that the harvest hereof, other hands shall reap."

11

Question: Murshid, you teach us to rise above all distinctions, and you give us distinction.

Answer: Yes, I give you something to rise above.

12

IN answer to the question to explain the idea of the scapegoat, Murshid said, "A master has the power to draw harmful magnetism from a person into his own body, which, by contact with his pure magnetism, is rendered harmless, thus freeing the man of a poison which would otherwise destroy him; and [this] is sometimes done in the case of an accepted disciple in whom a poisonous magnetism is in process of becoming active. If, however, the person has reached the stage when destruction of form has already begun, it may be a dangerous experiment for even a master to undertake the risk; and in that case he could, if necessity should arise, direct it from a human into an animal or less evolved form of life."

13

IT is safest to shut off all astral experiences until one is able to received spiritual knowledge. This is really a quicker way of progress in the end. To advance through each plane, mastering each as you go, is always full of danger, because one is held so long, examining much that is full of interest, that it may take millions of year to accomplish the journey.

14

[From Inayat Khan]

ADDRESS given after initiation:

My blessed mureed,

You have entered the path of service, but please understand that by *service* is meant not necessarily, nor generally, service to some church or organization, nor what is called *good works*. It is serving those nearest to us in any capacity, however insignificant it may seem, which is the real service of God; for that is the beginning of the injunction "to love thy neighbor as thyself."[1] So easy to say, so difficult to practice, even when it is realized that "All is One." Remember it is service, not knowledge, which takes an aspirant to the feet of God.

Blessings from Murshid.

1 Mark 12:31.

15

THERE is some work you must do before you can progress further; and if I were to do as you ask, to open your eyes to reality, you would be unable to finish your task. Your whole being would be so absorbed that you would be unfitted for physical world activity. The time is not yet. You would be dazed by the beauty; bewildered by the newness of thought and by having to change all your conceptions of things; so overwhelmed with wonder that you would be of no more use where you are.

The unfoldment of the mysteries must be a very gradual unfoldment if you would grow in strength and be complete. You might as well ask me to force open a rosebud and produce a perfect rose; only growth can do that. I am helping you to put forth the necessary strength for your own unfoldment. Have patience.

16

GO forward with a high courage; your desire shall be granted, have no fear. If a thing is right for you to do, then the way will be made easy; if not, you will be prevented. From this time onward your feet shall be guided; fear not, you may trust the guide, all is well. This is to instill into your mind the courage of the larger hope, which gives power to achieve great things. Don't be afraid, as I told you once before, to let your thoughts go with your desires and hope greatly; not your heart only, but your soul has seen. The heart knows, the soul knows; they can never doubt. It is only the mind that doubts. Your mind must be made to see also, that is why I have spoken tonight. There is much work to be done. You will need all your strength.

God bless you.

17

KEEP burning the fire I have lighted. It may seem very small to you, but one tiny flame, if kept burning, can be the means of illuminating a whole city. And some day many lamps that shall be lighted at this small fire will give light to thousands who are now in darkness. Guard it; tend it, day and night. All the winds of earth are trying to put it out, but they can never do this if you watch faithfully, and will rather cause it to burn more brightly. Watch and pray.

18

GO forward without regret, never once looking back; and remember that every sorrow and difficulty, and every joy, was a necessary experience to teach some lesson that had to be learned before you could tread the path that you have chosen. You will need great strength, great courage, and a great faith; but the reward is more than it has entered into the human heart to conceive: it is the joy of service, the fullness of joy, which can never be taken away.

19

HAVE you any idea of the sacredness of what you have been trusted with? I have put my life into you, and you have become a part of me. I have made myself responsible for all your actions, either good or bad; and in every action of your daily life, it is my force you are using. Your every action, thought or feeling is reflected on my heart; and your satisfaction or pain is my satisfaction and my pain. It is I who rejoice in your attainment, and I who am hurt when you fail.

20

OUR thoughts, and only our thoughts, make our real environment. Those who continually think about God are drawn to the great souls who sought God in all ages and became one with that wonderful fellowship of Illuminated Ones.

We cannot hold or be conscious of any ideal we ourselves have not created. We are all seeking the God we have created. At the end, we shall find, not God, but ourselves.

21

THE truth cannot be expressed in words. Suggestions only can be offered; each soul must seek the underlying truth for itself. This has been the experience of every true mystic.

The kingdom of heaven is within you. Do not look for Me, do not hope for Me outside yourself. Do not believe that I am outside of yourself. The abode of God is the human heart.

Yes, everything is possible when you have realized this great truth. An intellectual conception is not sufficient; true realization is a very different thing.

22

I CANNOT hold you back if you will go on. The only safety for you on this path is to keep your eyes fixed upon me.

Look neither to the right nor to the left; do not look up; and above all, do not look back; but [keep] your eyes always fixed on me and give me your utter trust. Only so I can take you through this way of bewilderment.

23

TRY to identify yourself with the ensouling force, not with the thing ensouled. So long as we identify ourselves with mind, we may say we reincarnate. What we must endeavor to do is to rise above mind and identify ourselves with spirit. That is the objective of the path to the goal: union with God, Who is Spirit.

24

ON the earth plane, the personality develops out of the individuality. The soul is an individual from the moment it is born upon earth, in the worldly sense of the word; but it becomes a phase as it grows. From personality, which is made by character-building, is born that spirit that is the rebirth of the soul. The first birth is the human birth, the next birth is the birth of God.

25

ONLY when the heart has become indifferent to pleasure or pain can the voice of the Beloved be heard.

26

ALTHOUGH necessary at a certain stage, it is not advisable for a disciple to depend upon the physical presence of the teacher, nor upon the teacher's spoken word; for the real teaching is not given by any physical means.

Not until the disciple has been accepted in the Beloved does the real teaching begin, which is for the purpose of opening the heart to perceive, with understanding, the vision of eternal Truth.

My mureeds are not only students. They are an army to fight the forces of darkness, which are trying to put out the forces of light.

No one is free from the forces of evil once one has set foot on the upwards path. But for your comfort, I would say there is joy in overcoming.

27

THOSE who shut themselves up from all humanity, even however high spiritual[ly] they may be, they will not be free in *malakut*.[1] In the higher spheres they will have round them a wall keeping away the genii from the spheres.

1 The celestial plane.

28

SPOKEN by God to the Bodhisattva:

"We have created thy light out of Our Spirit. If We had not created thee, We would not have created the whole universe."[1]

1 After the Hadith.

29

[From Hazrat Inayat Khan]

THE chief object of creation is the formation of the Bodhisattva.

The Lord Maitreya, the Bodhisattva Spirit, or Spirit of Guidance, working in man, fulfills his mission in a planet. On the fulfillment of his mission, he is crowned *Rasoul*.[1]

All the essence which rises from the intelligence of humanity merges into the Spirit of Guidance: the Bodhisattva; and all waste matter coming from the Spiritual of Guidance goes to make the intellect of man.

All masters and saints are group-souls. The souls belonging to a group-soul are not equal, but each is different and has a different purpose to fulfill. The master is not complete until all souls in the group are perfected.

Intelligence of humanity is the all-pervading, undifferentiated Spirit of God (Chaitanya).

---

1 *Rasoul* means a prophet. One in every cycle.

30

THE voice of God speaks through all things; but in order to awaken deaf ears, God uses the lips of human beings.

A Sufi must always recognize God as the source of all things and the origin of all beings.

A Sufi must observe, in the continual unfoldment of the spirit, the birth of soul.

31

THE best medicine is pure diet, regularity in sleep and action, fresh air, clear thinking, purity of feeling, and perfect confidence in the Divine Being with Whom we are linked and Whose essence we are.

If disease is the lack of life, how can one keep well?

By an intense realization of the presence of God, Who is Life; not by merely thinking about God, but a realization every moment of the day. To realize God means to become one with God, and so partake of God's Life, which will flood one's being and bring into harmony every part of our body.

32

THE sacred center of the heart is the organ or instrument of the higher self on the physical plane. When the heart center is open, the voice of the higher self can be heard.

Who has once sinned is a venturer; who has twice sinned is an explorer; but who has thrice sinned is a sinner.

By controlling one's sentiments, one becomes a reservoir of power.

33

THE pursuit after truth is more interesting than its attainment.

A service without wages, love without reciprocity, merit without [ ], beauty without appreciation.

Receive pain with resignation, and pleasure with thanksgiving.

34

WITHOUT humor, life is empty.

A verse without a twist is like an unflavored dish.

35

TO accuse a person of wickedness is a worse wickedness.

Forgiveness does not come by learning but by insight, by understanding that each one should be allowed to travel the path that is suited to one's temperament.

Action leads to perfection.

36

A SYMBOL is a resting place for the mind as it climbs the steps of reality.

37

[From Hazrat Inayat Khan]

EVERY man, on leaving this world, takes with him his own heaven or hell.

38

PEOPLE send through me a chill when they express to me their feelings against another.

39

[From Hazrat Inayat Khan]

SPIRITUALITY is a garb under which Satan hides and plays a role of a spiritual guide. For a time he will attract many by wonder-working, by being over-wise, by teaching superstitions, and by fascinating others by his false personality. He will make false promises and will give false hopes, will give false beliefs and will spread false doctrines. But the success of falsehood is momentary, and the success of truth is certain; for truth and success are not two things, they are one. There is as much likeness between falsehood and truth as there is between the person and his own shadow. The difference being that while the former has life, the latter has none. Where the body goes, there the shadow will go also. So the truth is followed by falsehood.

40

"TAKE, eat; this is my body."[1] These words of Jesus Christ are, as are all his inspired utterances, capable of many interpretations, for they contain a profound truth which can be perceived according to the power of perception of the seer.

Food, when eaten, or received into the physical body, ceases to be a substance separate and apart. It becomes one with the body it nourishes, part and indistinguishable from it. Without such nourishment a physical body could not exist, and all the bodies used by the human soul must likewise be nourished and sustained, each by its own substance. As the material body needs material food, and the mental body, mental food—knowledge of names and forms—so the spiritual body needs spiritual food: light.

Jesus the Christ said, "I am the Light of the world,"[2] and, "He that eateth me, even he shall live by me."[3] Whosover therefore eateth of the mystical body of Christ, his resurrection body of light, the Christ liveth in him, brought to birth in this sacrament of light. "Ye in me, and I in you,"[4] is the beginning of the at-one-ment; for the spirit of all men is one spirit: the One manifesting as many under various names and forms, seeds of light buried in darkness, which, in order to become alive and active, must be fed and nourished by their own substance.

1 Matthew 26:26.

2 John 8:12.

3 John 6:57.

4 John 14:20.

When all have been quickened, "The many return again to, and become one with, That from which they came forth."

> *The consciousness of the One Whole is the flesh of Christ, and the breath of love is his blood.*[5]
>
> *—Inayat Khan*

5 Inayat Khan, *The Gayan*.

41

YOU are mistaken in thinking that the sex-impulse is part of the animal side of the human being. On the contrary, it is the Divine Life in humanity and must not remain to stagnate and so upset life's rhythm; but coming from the Creator, [it] should flow in one unbroken chain through countless millions, and thus accomplish God's purpose to create and recreate, to build "Temples not made with hands"[1] for the Lord God to inhabit. When the sex-impulse is used for any other purpose than creation or recreation, then is its use wrong.

If sex-desire were not urgent in humans, God's purpose would be thwarted. It is the divine law, the natural unfoldment of humanity, that it should pass on the life, which is God's; and humanity's work on this globe is to build living forms in which God may express God's own Self.

1 Acts 7:48.

42

ACTION materializes spirit, stillness etherializes matter. Therefore, action is the process by which spirit can become matter, and stillness the process by which matter may turn into spirit.

Whoever knows the secret of life can transmute matter into spirit.

Sex-force is a process through which the unseen energy (ether) becomes a tangible substance. It, therefore, is a way through which spirit turns into matter. If the energy which has just become, or is on the way to become, a substance is transmuted, it joins the atoms of mind, thus making mind more powerful. The djinn part of a personality then becomes stronger than the human part. It is this that makes a person a genius.

If the love, or motion, towards one of the opposite sex is conserved and transmuted upwards, it strengthens the human spirit, making a person fit for service to humanity. The method of transmutation is by concentration, contemplation, meditation, and relaxation.

43

THE greatest problem of the world will be solved on the day when woman will not be man's own property, and man will not be counted among woman's belongings.

44

THE God-ideal is the best ideal that human mind can ever create.

Create heaven or hell, whatever you may; both are your own creation.

If humanity would have been perfect, there had been no God.

Sin is the stepping-stone to virtue.

If you are displeased with yourself, then the whole world, even God, is displeased with you. But if you are really satisfied with yourself, then what else do you need?

45

WHEN you rise above passion, you know what is love;
When you rise above love, you know what is God;
But when you rise above God, you will know yourself.

46

IF not saint, Satan; take some model to mold your life on.

The spirit in its limitation is devil; in its perfection is God.

God is perfected in human personality.

You cannot love the God of reality; you can only love the God you have made.

47

POETIC inspiration is just like a stream of water: it cannot be stopped, it will make its way.

48

THE secret of life and death is to be found in the mystery of breath.

49

PROPHECIES:

The end of the world will be brought about by the advanced mechanical inventions.

Ships will fly; houses will fly.

The children of the future will be the children of a community.

All nations will be governed by one government.

Spirituality will overpower materiality.

Wisdom will conquer religion.

Communism will culminate in spiritualism.

Marriage will go out of fashion.

Home-life will cease to exist.

The life of the world will become every day more mechanical.

The conveniences and comforts of humanity in general will be linked up by one mechanism, which will produce comforts and conveniences beyond human imagination. But the smallest mistake will bring the whole mechanism to a certain collapse. In this way the end of the world will be brought about.

Human brotherhood will develop.

Aristocracy will fade away; democracy will degenerate.

Commonwealth will become the principle of nations. A world commonwealth will be the ideal of nations.

May 12, 1922

50

MEANING of Numbers:

1 = spiritual perfection; no effect on physical things.
2 = success in action on the physical plane; kindness and illusion.
3 = spiritual realization.
4 = justice or settlement.
5 = perfection.
6 = illumination and destruction.
7 = harmony.
8 = worldly law; absence of progress
9 = progressive [sic] or continuation.
10 = perfection.

1 = freedom and purification.
2 = beauty and balance.
3 = life and production.
4 = settlement and strength.
5 = creation and sustenance.
6 = divisions.
7 = harmony.
8 = balance and fortification.
9 = progress and amplification.
10 = perfection.

51

THERE are seven planes:

First plane: the original designer.
Three planes where the designs are made.
Three planes where they are colored.

Aspects of mind:

memory, reason, ego, creative mind, conscience.

A Biographical Portrait of the Author

by Nancy Barta-Norton

Nargis Jessie Dowland

JESSIE Eliza Dowland (1866–1953), whose spiritual name was Nargis, was a pupil (*mureed*) and representative of Hazrat Inayat Khan in England. Until recently, her spiritual legacy was not as well-known or documented as that of Inayat Khan's "four Murshidas"[1]: Rabia Ada Martin, Sharifa Lucy Goodenough, Sophia Saintsbury-Green, and Fazl Mai Petronella Egeling—all of whom made unique and important contributions to the unfoldment of the Message in our time.[2]

As reflected in her substantial body of published and unpublished writings, Nargis' special gift was her deeply mystical understanding of the path of discipleship and the Spirit of Guidance, and her high degree of spiritual sensitivity, allowing an *uwaisi*-type of relationship with her murshid, Inayat Khan.[3] Recognizing this special attunement, in a letter dated January 3, 1922, Inayat Khan suggests she adopt the pen name

1 The title *murshid* (from the Persian) signifies a senior teacher or guide in the spiritual tradition of the Sufis.

2 Brief biographies of these four murshidas can be found in Pir Zia Inayat-Khan's, *Caravan of Souls: An Introduction to the Sufi Path of Hazrat Inayat Khan* (New Lebanon: Suluk Press, 2013) 61–67.

3 Uwaisi transmissions are direct sharings of spiritual knowledge that can occur without the physical presence of the teacher; they can also be transmissions or initiations from a deceased teacher to a living student. The term is derived from Uwais al-Qarni of Yemen, who was said to have communicated with the Prophet Muhammad on a heart level without ever having the opportunity of meeting him physically. Of him, the Prophet would say, "I feel the breath of the Merciful, coming to me from Yemen."

Nargis, "which means *Narcis*, symbolically, 'inspired soul whose heart is focused on the Spirit of Guidance.'" Subsequently, she signed her books "inscribed by Nargis, pupil of Inayat Khan" and also penned a series of sayings on the spiritual life, which she described as "Murshid's inner teaching as received in the silence and rendered by Nargis." As the title page of her book *Between the Desert and the Sown: The Way of the Disciple* reveals, her primary aim in writing was to share "some practical teachings for aspirants to discipleship,"[4] this turn of phrase revealing her view of the spiritual path as a journey toward an ever-receding horizon. While maintaining a high level of worldly responsibility as the manager of the Polygon House Hotel in Southampton, and also as National Representative of the Sufi Movement in England (1921–1933), she found a way to live a deeply mystical inner life through her profound connection with her teacher.

Very little is known about Jessie Dowland's early life and education. She was born in Richmond, Surrey, England, in the first quarter of 1866.[5] No information is available on Jessie's biological mother in extant genealogical records. Her father, Frederick Dowland, was described as "an architect, deceased" on Jessie's death certificate;[6] however, the 1861 census describes him as a nineteen-year old apprentice auctioneer living with his mother in Lee, St. Margaret, Kent.[7] His father, also named Frederick (b. 1820), is not included as a household member in that same census of 1861. In 1865 in Windsor, at the age of twenty-three, Frederick married nine-

4 Dowland, Nargis, *Between the Desert and the Sown: The Way of the Disciple.* (Southampton: Sufi Movement, 1923), cover page.

5 *England & Wales, Free BMD Birth Index, 1837–1915.* (Provo: Ancestry.com, 2006). Jessie's birth is registered with the births in January, February and March, 1866 (Vol. 2a, p. 274).

6 "Certified Copy of an Entry of Death." (Southampton: Dec. 31, 1953, no. 386). See also *England & Wales Death Index, 1916–2007* (Provo: Ancestry.com, 2007).

7 *Census Returns of England and Wales, 1861.* (Provo: Ancestry.com, 2005).

teen year old Sophie Dowland (c.1846–1929), who two years later gave birth to their son, Douglas F. Dowland (1867–1927), Jessie's half-brother.[8] By the time of the 1871 census, Mr. and Mrs. Dowland, three-year old Douglas, and their domestic appear to have taken residence in Lambeth, London. There are many ambiguities and gaps in the recorded family history after this, with no completely reliable information available on Frederick from his thirties onward. However, according to the 1881 census, Sophie and her son Douglas were "visiting" with John H. and Emily C. Hardy (most likely her sister, also born in Windsor, Berkshire); and Sophie was employed as a teacher of singing in Lambeth. In 1901, Sophie, now fifty-five, is a "widow," and she is again "visiting" with Albert L. and Beatrice Underwood in Lee, London.[9]

It is clear that young Jessie was not a member of Frederick and Sophie Dowland's Lambeth household. According to English census records, in 1871, at age five, Jessie was living with her fifty-one-year old grandmother, Eliza Cook Dowland, a retired upholsterer, and her grandmother's niece, Emma Cheffer (b. 1850) in Lee, Kent, England. In 1881, at age fifteen, she was still residing with her now sixty-one-year old widowed grandmother, who was then occupied as a lodging house keeper, and a domestic servant at 22 Chatham Place, Brighton, Sussex. By the time of the 1901 census, Jessie was listed as the single, 35-year old manageress of The Polygon House Hotel in Southampton.[10]

The circumstances of Jessie's initial encounter with Inayat Khan have not been documented. In a brief biographical sketch of Nargis found in Inayat Khan's biography, it is remarked that she "seems to have been an efficient and capable manager" of the Polygon House Hotel who, after her initiation in 1919,

8 "Sophie Dowland." (Provo: Ancestry.com).

9 *Census Returns of England and Wales, 1871, 1881, 1901* (Provo: Ancestry.com, 2005).

10 Ibid.

"put this same efficiency also into the work for the Sufi Order and Movement in England."[11]

Nargis' inspirational, beautifully crafted compositions indicate that she was well-educated and that she read widely. On the basis of the many references found in her writings, it is clear that Jessie Dowland gave a close reading to the Old and New Testaments of the Bible and that she was strongly attracted to the sayings of Jesus, including the apocryphal *Logia* discovered in 1897, today known as *The Gospel of Thomas.* She cited Eastern and Western poets and literary figures such as Johann Wolfgang von Goethe, Matthew Arnold, Robert Browning, Shakespeare, and Muhammad Iqbal; philosophers such as Abelard and Ralph Waldo Emerson; mystics such as the Buddha, Kabir and Angelus Silesius; contemporary spiritual thinkers such as Evelyn Underhill and Lily Adams Beck, and others, for example, H.G. Wells and Louis Pasteur. She often included quotations from Sufis, including Omar Khayyam, Abu Said Ibn Abi'l Khair, Jalal ad-Din Rumi, Shams Tabriz, Kwajja Bayazid, Sharaf al-Din Maneri, and, of course, frequently quoted from the works of her own teacher, Inayat Khan. Beyond this, she possessed more than a passing familiarity with world scriptures, ranging from the more familiar Judeo-Christian scriptures to the Tao Teh Ching and Bhagavad Gita. Her knowledge of Theosophy is also in evidence, as she quotes Madame H. P. Blavatsky in her writings and enjoyed a close friendship with Murshida Sophia Saintsbury-Green, whom Inayat Khan describes as "a Theosophist for most of her life, a special pupil of Mrs. Besant, and who through Theosophy came to recognize the Truth sent in the Sufi Message."[12] It is quite likely that Nargis moved in the

11 "Biographical Sketch of Miss Jessie Eliza Dowland (Khalifa Nargis)," *Biography of Pir-o-Murshid Inayat Khan* (London: East-West Publications, 1979), 496.

12 Inayat Khan, *Autobiography*. 149. Sophia Saintsbury-Green (d. 1939) was one of Inayat Khan's early pupils. A writer and poet, she is best known for her *Images of Inayat,* revised edition (New Lebanon: Suluk

same Theosophical circles as Murshida Green, one of Inayat Khan's primary workers in England.

Moreover, Nargis possessed an unfailing ear for the cadences of language. In her writing, one hears echoes of the prophetic books, the gospels, and the parables. One also finds a clear reflection of Inayat Khan's manner of speech and phraseology.

The correspondence between Hazrat Inayat Khan and Nargis spanning the years 1921–1926 clearly demonstrates her instrumental role in providing material support for her murshid and in accelerating the growth of the Sufi Movement in England. Inayat consistently addresses her as "My dear and very trusted mureed," or "my blessed and trusted mureed" in his letters, sometimes calling her his *khalifa*, or sometimes *shaikha* (or *shaika*), designating her spiritual rank in the Esoteric School. In the *Autobiography*, Inayat states, "Differences among my loving friends threatened our movement with a breakdown and caused the removal of the Khankah to Geneva. At that critical moment, Miss Dowland came to its rescue, and our infant Order was given into her arms when leaving England, recognizing in her the hand of God."[13] After appointing her National Representative of the Order in England (1921–1933), Inayat Khan notes, "Her capacity in working had made the Order increase in members, in organization much better than before."[14] Moreover, Nargis helped Inayat overcome what he had termed his "bitterest enemy": poverty. He states, "Miss Dowland brought into existence that fund which was intended to be for my maintenance, and continued it for three years, when it was sorely

---

Press, 2014), in which there is a profile of the author by Suria Rebecca McBride. In it, Sophia Saintsbury-Green shares some memories and impressions of Inayat Khan.

13 Note salutations used by Inayat throughout the collection, Letters by Hazrat Inayat Khan to Miss (Shaikha) Dowland and (Khalifa) Murshida Green (1921–1927). Despite the title of this manuscript, Miss Dowland was most often addressed as "Khalifa" and Miss Green as "Murshida"). The quote from Inayat can be found in the *Autobiography*, 149.

14 Inayat Khan, *Autobiography*, 149

needed. Later the same fund was also subscribed to by the mureeds from Holland, Belgium, and Switzerland."[15] In his letters, he frequently thanks her for the small but thoughtful comforts she provided for him and for his family: the black leather purse given to him on his birthday, books and magazines, some favorite butter biscuits, a chest protector, gifts for his children and the Begum (Inayat's American wife, Ora Ray Baker), as well as food for his family's table at Christmas; she also lent her support to his cousin, Ali Khan. Inayat was also deeply grateful for his "seat" at the Polygon Hotel and his stays in small rural lodgings in the New Forest.[16]

Inayat Khan frequently expressed profound gratitude for Nargis' material support, but even more so for her understanding and unflagging dedication to the cause, saying "How thankful I am to have a sympathetic mureed like [you] who wishes to save me from every trouble, and that is the proof of you having insight into my life. How difficult it is in the world to get a person who understands, for the understanding person is greater than the one who loves or admires"; this is reminiscent of his saying from *The Bowl of Saki*: "He who loves is a devotee, but he who understands is a friend."[17] Elsewhere, Inayat says, "I do not find proper expression to thank you for your many kindnesses; if it was one, I could mention it, but it is in so many forms that you show your devotion, faithfulness, and sympathy with your Murshid."[18] On her part, Nargis wrote to her murshid, "I am very well and in spite of all the difficulties feel quite happy and peaceful, except that I do not know how you are situated and whether you are needing anything. Will you give me your confidence

15 "Personal Account," *Biography of Pir-o-Murshid Inayat Khan*. 185.

16 Inayat Khan, letters to Miss Dowland, 1922; Apr. 1922; May 17, 1922; Dec. 1922; Liege, Belgium; 1924 (before May); May 13, 1924; July 17, 1924, and Sept. 17 1924.

17 Inayat Khan, letter to Miss Dowland, Mar. 1, 1921; Inayat Khan, *The Bowl of Saki*, July 29.

18 Inayat Khan, letter to Miss Dowland, Dec. 27, 1923.

and tell me which way I can help most? . . . My earnest desire is to do whatever will help to spread the Message in the way *you* wish most, even if this means that you have to be away from us . . . While life lasts, I shall never be able to show my gratitude for all you have done for me and can only hope to show it in some small measure by service."[19]

Nargis' life was indeed one of great responsibility and service. She never married, but had considerable administrative obligations at a time when this was not so common for women. As a "manageress" of the Polygon House Hotel[20] her duties were numerous and pressing. The Polygon, originally constructed in the eighteenth century and reconstructed in the 1870s, was the most famous hotel in Southampton, setting high standards in hospitality and attracting many celebrity guests over the years. Nargis' responsibilities prevented her from attending the Sufi Summer School in Europe or an Executive Council meeting held in Geneva (1921), where Mumtaz Armstrong represented England in her absence.[21]

19 "Biographical Sketch of Miss Jessie Eliza Dowland (Khalifa Nargis)," *Biography of Pir-o-Murshid Inayat Khan.* 496.

20 Elizabeth de Jong-Keesing describes her role as "owner" of the hotel. de Jong-Keesing, Elizabeth, *Inayat Khan: A Biography.* (The Hague: East-West Publications, 1974), 164. As described by Peter Neal in *The Story of Southampton* (Gloucestershire: History Press, 2014), the Polygon House Hotel was originally part of the so-called "Polygon development scheme" initiated in 1768, an attempt to make Southampton an attractive resort/spa venue emulating Bath's Golden Crescent. Over twenty acres with views of the water and New Forest were designated for the Polygon project. Jacob Leroux, the architect, envisioned construction of "a circle of twelve grand houses surrounding an inner section, which would contain a hotel and shops" (76). A "most magnificent hotel" was built on this site, opening in 1773, but it suffered from the downscaling of the initial Polygon plan and competition with other hotels, such as the Dolphin, sited within the town precincts; Neal reports that, lacking buyers, this hotel was demolished (p.78). According to the PortCities website, parts of the original hotel were incorporated into a new hotel built in the 1870s; the hotel was once again rebuilt in the 1930s, then ultimately demolished in 1999, with luxury apartments being built on the site (see PortCities: Southampton): http://www.plimsoll.org/resources/SCCLibraries/2657.asp

21 Inayat Khan, letter to Miss Dowland, Oct. 7. 1921

Nevertheless, in her role as England's National Representative, she was occupied with the Sufi work in many capacities, including fundraising and publishing.

In his letters to Nargis, Inayat Khan constantly sends his thoughts and blessings, along with his inquiries about the health and well-being of her "mother." Though there is no exact information on her date of death, Eliza Cook Dowland, the grandmother who had mothered and raised Jessie, was eighty-one and living "on her own means in a boarding house" in Hove, Sussex, England by the time of the 1901 census.[22] Her date of death, likely in Hove, is uncertain, but if alive she would have been very advanced in age by the time of Nargis' correspondence with Inayat Khan (1921–1926). Was the "mother" referred to in these letters her father's wife, Sophie Dowland, who in 1929, when she died at the age of eighty-three, is known to have been residing in Southampton? In either case, the correspondence suggests that in addition to her managerial obligations and her duties related to the Sufi Order, Nargis had family care-giving responsibilities.

Nargis also seems to have been closely involved in the life of her half-brother, Douglas, who, unlike Jessie, had married, on February 12, 1901 in Christ Church, Holborn, Camden. His wife, Lilian Maude (Spurrier) Church, was the daughter of Henry and Elizabeth Spurrier, keepers of the Sun Hotel, 85 High Street in Chatham. At the time of her marriage to Douglas, Lilian was a widow with a young son, Roy Church. It appears that Douglas, with the assistance of his wife Lilian, later took up the occupation of hotel keeper at the same Sun Hotel; his occupations are variously described as "Spirit Trav-

22 Hazrat Inayat Khan, letters to Miss Dowland: March 1, 1921; Oct. 7 and 13, 1921, 1921 [Weimar, Germany]; 1922 [Wissous]; May 17, 1922; April 2, 1923; December 27, 1923; S at.,1924 (before May); May 13, 1924; Liege, Belgium; July 17, 1924; Sept 17, 1924; Dec. 29, 1926; although the addressee is uncertain, possibly also Oct. 3, 1925, Dec. 25, 1925, Jan. 9, 1926, Autumn 1926. See also *Census Returns of England and Wales, 1901* (Provo: Ancestry.com, 2005) and "Eliza Cook." (Provo: Ancestry.com).

eller," (1901 Census) or "Spirit Merchant (1901 Marriages and Banns) and "Hotel Keeper" (1911 Census).[23]

In his correspondence with Nargis, Inayat Khan inquires about her brother. From her letters, we can also see that Nargis has mentioned some special intention of her nephew's to her murshid, who prays in order that "some way is opened" for him—and later remarks he is "glad" for him when this intention is presumably fulfilled. Acutely aware of the heavy demands of leadership in the Order and knowing their close connection, Inayat Khan also charges Nargis with monitoring the well-being of her good friend and spiritual associate, Murshida Sophia Saintsbury-Green, saying "I hope Murshida is enjoying good health; she must be looked aftr [sic]" and also "Upon her well being much depends."[24]

In their correspondence, Nargis and Inayat Khan also engaged in considerable discussion of organizational and business matters pertaining to the Order: travel and scheduling arrangements, and details of the publishing venture, from content to pricing. Clearly, he was very open to her suggestions and advice regarding ways to proceed with his work in England and trusted her judgment in matters pertaining to publications. Beyond that, it is evident that Inayat Khan found in Nargis a valued and highly esteemed confidante with whom he could share remarkably candid observations on the many difficulties, large and small, connected with his mission. He speaks openly to her of rivalries and disputes within the ranks that affect his "tranquility and peace of mind"; he also bemoans the "critical world" whose "work in

---

23 *London, England, Marriages and Banns, 1754-1921*. (Provo: Ancestry.com, 2010); *Census Returns of England and Wales, 1901* (Provo: Ancestry.com, 2005); *Census Returns of England and Wales, 1911* (Provo: Ancestry.com, 2011). "Public Houses, Inns & Taverns of Chatham, Kent" (http://pubshistory.com/KentPubs/Chatham/SunHotel.shtml).

24 Inayat Khan, letters to Miss Dowland, Oct. 7, 1921; 1921 [Weimar, Germany]; Sept. 17, 1924; Saturday 1924 (Before May); also (addressee uncertain) Oct. 3, 1925.

life is to criticize [while] our work in life is to work, and let us see who sins in the end."[25] At one point, he states, "The difficulties of [the] general working of the Order has [sic] nearly turned all my hair grey. The chief difficulty is money to sustain myself and to keep the headquarters living, which is to be the spiritual kitchen for the whole world"; furthermore, he notes that there is "no end of demands upon my time, every blessed moment is taken up in something or another" and "however much I work it is never enough."[26] Inayat repeatedly expresses his appreciation for Nargis' unfailing help and support, for her consoling letters, during these challenging moments; of this, he says, "We cannot open our heart to everybody and show the wound."[27] With longtime professional experience attending to the comfort of her hotel guests, coupled with her deep spiritual sensitivity and strong desire to serve her teacher and the cause, Nargis was able to provide welcome rest and respite for Inayat Khan while he was in England, and especially when staying at the Polygon.

Within the many constraints and demands imposed by Nargis' life circumstances and his own overfilled calendar, Inayat Khan found ways to work with his busy mureed. The following passage can be found in Nargis' previously unpublished notebook: "Murshid used to say to Miss Dowland, 'I impart in you my light, my life, my strength, my power, my joy, and my peace.' As her busy life did not allow her much time for meditation, this was one way in which Inayat Khan helped and trained her: to remember and repeat these words every time before going to bed. Inayat Khan also said to her, 'Be content to know nothing, to be nothing; just give me your service.'"[28] In addition to this phrase for concentration, he prescribed repetition of particular *wazaif* (Names of God) for her personal needs, and in response to her request for a

25 Inayat Khan, letters to Miss Dowland, Oct. 7, 1921 and Mar. 14, 1921.

26 Inayat Khan, letters to Miss Dowland, Sept. 14, 1921 and 1921 [Brussels].

27 Inayat Khan, letter to Miss Dowland, 1922 [Wissous].

28 *Miss Dowland's Notebook* (London, 1919–1927).

spiritual practice to "help to settle the Publishing Society's difficulties"; at one point, he asks her "Shall we pray at the same time for nine consecutive days?" and he tells her "I always pray for you in the midst of the night."[29] Murshid's unwavering support, concern, guidance, and subtle ways of working with her are always evident.

By Nargis' own description, her path was entirely one of devotion, surrender, and trust: "Devotion is the only bridge by which a soul can safely pass from one state of being to another, and each soul must evolve his own bridge from himself, as the spider spins from its own body the thread by which it cross from one place to another; no one can cross over on the bridge of another; each man's path is within himself and for himself alone."[30] Especially in those "inner teachings" which she received "in the silence," Nargis reveals a profound understanding of the relationship between the Murshid and the mureed in an undated teaching, "The Tie":

> *The tie between a murshid and mureed is a very close and sacred tie, for he becomes responsible not only for any good action but for every failing and shortcoming of an accepted disciple, and in his own body must readjust all that becomes unbalanced.*
>
> *This does not mean that the mureed is no more responsible for his acts; he should feel doubly responsible when he realizes that every act of his life, not big things only, but the ordinary everyday things of life are reflected in the heart of his murshid and will cause him joy or pain.*
>
> *The murshid tunes his accepted mureed to a particular note and can feel every vibration, so if you desire to make easier the path of the murshid remember the sacred trust that has been given you and so live your life that only harmonious vibrations may reach him.*

29 Inayat Khan, letters to Miss Dowland, 1921 [Weimar, Germany]; Sept. 14, 1921.

30 "Virtues," an unpublished inner teaching received in the silence by Nargis Dowland.

> *As the mureed learns to still his own mind, so will he be able to receive and understand the vibrations sent to him from his murshid.*[31]

Despite numerous obstacles, Nargis' dedication and deep attunement were such that Inayat Khan wrote to her, "When you are not present in the physical plane, you are here in spirit. You are coming closer every day to your Murshid."[32]

Nargis did share at least two occasions of extraordinary grace and sacredness with Inayat Khan and her friend Murshida Sophia Saintsbury-Green in the New Forest, a wooded area adjacent to Southampton. One of these occurred in 1919, the year that Nargis received initiation, the other in the summer of 1920. These moments outside of time made an indelible impression upon her spirit, and she treasured them always. In her own words, Nargis describes one of these mystical New Forest sojourns in her notebook:

> *Once I had a concert at the Polygon Hotel and Murshid sang with the vina different songs. I never saw Murshid alone in the Hotel, and I wanted to see him alone. I took a taxi and sought in the 'New Forest' for [a] place. At last I found a small hotel, and by the side of it was a little annex. There were two sitting rooms and a very large kitchen, three bedrooms, and a room with a bath in it. I took that on May 31st till June 3rd, 1919. It was called 'New Forest Inn.' It was in Emery Down. After the concert we just got into a taxi, Murshid, Murshida Green and myself, and we drove there. On a Saturday, I think. While we were there, Murshid took the vina in the middle of the Forest. We sat on a rug and we were quite alone. We sat for hours in the morning and spoke. And Murshid sang and we did not know where we were. It was like Omar Khayyam says, 'To-morrow? Why, to-morrow I may be myself with yesterday's seven thousand years.' We had to come to Southampton for a lecture on Sunday. On the Monday we went into the Forest. Murshid said,*

31 Dowland, Nargis, "The Tie," an unpublished inner teaching.

32 Inayat Khan, letter to Miss Dowland, Summer School [1924].

> *'Now we will take one day out of eternity.' A telegram came that Mamuli was born [this was his daughter and youngest child, Khairunnisa, born Tuesday, June 3, 1919]. We went back by taxi."*[33]

Murshida Green described a second visit to the New Forest:

> *On Tuesday, August 17th, 1920, I stayed with Aimee [her term of affection for Ms. Dowland] and Murshid at Woodlands, Emery Down, Hampshire. Murshid did not talk much in his usual way of teaching as he was much occupied with decisions about the Headquarters of the Movement. On Tuesday we all walked in the forest and in the most beautiful part we stood still in an absolute silence of nature. Suddenly a small wind rose from just behind us, and every tree and shrub bent and rustled and then began to be violently agitated. Murshid made a slight gesture and spoke one word very low, the word I believe to have been "Allah," and on the instant there was utter stillness. The wind neither came from a distance nor passed away beyond us; it rose and fell immediately where we stood. When we came in Miss Dowland asked him what the little wind was and he said, "It was a very important moment; there are Initiations on every plane." Again, he said, "This place will be historical; important events are happening on the astral plane."*
>
> *On the day he was leaving for town, Miss Dowland asked him if this time during which we had been with him had not been an Initiation. He replied, "Yes, and a very high Initiation."*[34]

In *Inayat Khan: A Biography*, Elizabeth de Jong-Keesing relates Inayat's love of walking and playing his vina in the "enchanted silence" of New Forest. She supplies an alternate description of an incident which took place there, likely that same 1920 visit recalled by Murshida Green:

---

33 Dowland, Nargis, *Miss Dowland's Notebook*,

34 Saintsbury-Green, Sophia, unpublished account.

> *In the middle of a conversation with two companions the Master suddenly hurried on ahead, showing a certain restlessness, as in Katwijk. But this time the disciples stayed with him and witnessed the moment of upliftment; they saw that nature responded too, as Inayat had seen when he met the muni in the Himalayas. He himself recalls this event in one of his letters: "I cannot forget the most worshipful time in the forest."*[35]

Nargis treasured the extraordinary experiences she was privileged to share with Murshid for the rest of her life, pondering them in her heart. In an unpublished transcript from a mureed's seminar dated November 24, 1979, Pir Vilayat Inayat Khan recalled a conversation he had with a then elderly Miss Dowland, in which she recounted something of her time in the New Forest:

> *And I remember very well hearing from Miss Dowland, who was an old mureed of the time of Murshid. I spoke to her during the Second World War, before she died. And she told me that Murshid had stayed in a sort of boarding house . . . in the New Forest in England. And [he] was really doing a retreat, and he would walk a lot and sit under the trees and meditate. And one day, she knocked at the door, because she kept waiting and waiting for some sign of life, and he didn't seem to stir. So she knocked again, and then eventually she opened the door, and there was Murshid sitting in meditation. She didn't want to disturb him, so she sat there for some time, and then it was getting so long, and so she went*

35 de Jong Keesing, Elizabeth, *Inayat Khan: A Biography* (The Hague: East West Publications, 1974), 188-189; "Hazrat Inayat Khan, letter to Ms. Dowland, May 17, 1922." De Jong Keesing refers to a profound spiritual experience Inayat Khan had in the dunes of Katwijk (1922), which he later called *Murad Hassil*, a place of fulfillment of desires; subsequently, a Universel or Sufi Temple was built nearby while the site of Inayat's experience was preserved as a place of contemplation and silence. In some correspondence from London dated April 1922 {?], Inayat Khan also says, "I enjoyed my stay in the forest; indeed, it was so helpful and uplifting at this time."

> *on her lunch. And then she knocked again in the afternoon, and there he was sitting. And then, the next day, he was still sitting there. And he hadn't moved. And then she was getting very, very worried. She was wondering if she should call the doctor.*
>
> *And it was only on the fourth day that Murshid started showing signs of moving a little bit—his hands a little bit, his eyes were half opened. It took many, many hours before he was able to walk at all, and then very slowly, and with some difficulty. And he couldn't speak. And then, eventually, he started speaking. And he said he had relived the whole past of the universe, and . . . he saw into the future, and it was a kind of Messianic vision of the whole, the meaning of life, and of course, it was entering into the Divine Consciousness.*[36]

Apart from her energetic support of Inayat Khan and the fledgling Order in England, Nargis' special contributions were most evident in two other areas: in the genesis of the Universal Worship service and in publication efforts. Along with her written contributions of poems, essays, and teachings "received in the silence" to the *Sufi* journal, Nargis published Inayat Khan's lectures and also produced several books and pamphlets sharing her own insights on the path of discipleship.

From passages in her notebook (c1921), we see that Nargis engaged Inayat Khan in discussion of the religious ceremonies and forms within Sufism, leading to the creation of one of the five activities of the Sufis, the Universal Worship. She recounts one of these discussions, written in the third person:

> *Once when Murshid was standing with Miss Dowland before a dilapidated old Church, Miss Dowland said to him, "Oh Murshid, shouldn't we buy this and rebuild it for the Sufis?" Murshid answered, "Never, never, never will Murshid found a Church." A week later Murshid dictated to her at*

36 Inayat Khan, Pir Vilayat, unpublished transcript (Mureed's Meeting, Nov. 24, 1979).

> *her flat in Southampton the* Service of the Universal Worship. *It was then and there that the* Church of All *came into existence.*
>
> *Murshid told her that all the attendants of the Service should sit on the floor. "Very well, Murshid," she answered, "but then nobody will come." After this, they were allowed to sit on chairs.*[37]

Professor Donald (Sharif Munawwir) Graham, in his article "The First Universal Worship Service," describes in detail the genesis of the Universal Worship, one of the five activities of the Sufi Order (the other activities being the Esoteric School; Brotherhood, now known as Kinship; the Healing Order; and Ziraat). The service, which he tells us was held at 35 Tregunter Road in London, the home of Gladys I. Lloyd, occurred on May 7, 1921. In this article, Graham quotes an anonymous attendee as saying:

> *At Southampton, Pir-o-Murshid found those who were to be true support and strength of the Message and channels for its furtherance. It is believed that the master had hoped that a certain celebrated esoteric society would be ready to receive him, but it only offered a platform for some lectures, so a fresh organization had to be started to launch the Message with its activities. Pir-o-Murshid appointed Miss Dowland of Southampton the National Representative of England and ordained Miss Saintsbury-Green the first Cheraga ["lamp," the title for an officiant of the Universal Worship]. She was first to help Pir-o-Murshid in founding the Church of All (the Universal Worship), the religious activity of the movement, and the details of the service were thought out and settled upon in Miss Dowland's sitting room (in Southampton) before the inaugural ceremony, which took place during a three week visit to London in May 1921.*[38]

---

37 Dowland, Nargis, *Miss Dowland's Notebook.*

38 Graham, Donald Avery (Sharif Munawwir), "The First Universal Worship Service," Aug. 18, 2006. Accessed at: http://www.universalworship.eu/the-universal-worship-service/the-first-universal-worship-service/.

In the same paper, Graham quotes Shabaz Mitchell, "a professional journalist from Southampton," who describes that service, expertly capturing the atmosphere of beauty and sacredness of that day. Mitchell describes the special role that Nargis Dowland played in the first Universal Worship service:

> *Murshid stands facing his mureeds and Miss Dowland, the National Representative, on his left hand begins to read the prayers in a calm, strong voice. As she reads, Murshid, with closed eyes, makes gently and with deliberation the appropriate gestures, his movements being watched by all with indescribable emotion. The prayers themselves are the most comprehensive we have ever listened to; they lift the thoughts to things above and turn them on things beneath.*[39]

Graham adds, "The fact that Murshid himself performed the gestures as Nargis Dowland recited the prayers shows that he felt the movements were most important." Six mureeds participated in the Reception into the Church of All ceremony, the core members of the Church of All. He also notes that Inayat Khan attached great significance to this moment, as reflected in his comment "the body of the movement is formed today."[40]

The friendship of Murshida Saintsbury-Green and Khalifa Dowland, so evident in their sojourns with Inayat Khan in the New Forest, can also be sensed in the collaborative planning sessions for that first Universal Worship, which took place in Nargis' Southampton home in advance of the London ceremony. One can readily imagine the affectionate partnership of these two mureeds in crafting every detail of the service with their murshid. In Nargis, one finds a mystical disposition, deep insight, and an attraction to religious symbolism balanced with an unassuming dependability and effectiveness, quiet strength, and deep dedication to service. When

39 Ibid.

40 Ibid.

speaking of Murshida Saintsbury-Green, Pir Vilayat describes a woman of "great intelligence" and "great power of expression," who had "penetrated into the spirit of the Message" and "had a gift for expressing it in words which turned people on and was able to arouse overwhelming enthusiasm." In her, he found "a perfect blend between realization and expression," and recalls that whenever she gave a sermon "you could never find a hall that was big enough for her; the people used to flock and stay outside in the street."[41] In his correspondence of 1921–1927, Inayat Khan frequently mentions these two friends in the same breath, an indication of their close personal and working relationship. The dynamic complementarity of these two friends, as first Cheraga and National Representative, helped to shape the Church of All and facilitated the growth and development of the Sufi work in England.

Another area in which Nargis played a critical role was publications. Early efforts had been made to disseminate the teachings of Inayat Khan in England, led by a mureed named Zohra Williams:

> *In order to publish literature as we liked, we started a Sufi Publishing Society in England, which was given into the charge of Miss Williams, who brought out a book of some ideas from my lectures, called,* Pearls from the Ocean Unseen. *Besides the work she did as sub-editor of the Sufi Magazine, she has been a sincere and devoted mureed and a most enthusiastic worker for the Cause. By this Publishing Society my poetical works were brought out,* Diwan, Hindustani Lyrics, *and* the Songs of India, *which were rendered into English by Mrs. Jessie Duncan Westbrook. My* Confessions *were published, written by Miss Miriam Bloch, a treatise on the* Rubaiyat of Omar Khayyam *by Mr. Bjerregaard was also published by this society.*[42]

41 Inayat Khan, Pir Vilayat, unpublished transcript (Cherag's Camp, Abode of the Message, Aug. 1980), 2.

42 Inayat Khan, "Autobiography," *Biography of Pir-o-Murshid Inayat*

In his *Autobiography*, Inayat Khan credits Nargis with the revival of efforts to publish his lectures:

> *The Sufi Publishing Society, which was dying away, was made alive by Miss Dowland, who called it the* Sufi Book Depot, *and brought out* The Bowl of Saki, The Message, The Inner Life, The Alchemy of Happiness, The Mysticism of Sound *and* Notes of the Unstruck Music, *and* The Soul Whence and Whither . . . *The self-sacrificing devotion with which Miss Dowland has worked in England will always remain in the history of the work of the Order in England. Those who have assisted Sheikha Dowland in her work concerning the Order are the Misses Wiseman, Miss Wentworth Sheilds (Cheraga) and Mr. Mitchell (Cherag).*[43]

In addition to her efforts to publish her murshid's words, Nargis also had a number of exquisite original writings of her own, published in the *Sufi* and *Sufism* journals, as pamphlets, and as monographs, elaborating on the nature of spiritual discipleship. Wil van Beek reports that Nargis "gained great popularity in Sufi and related circles" and also that she "injected new life into the Sufi Publishing Society."[44] In his correspondence with Nargis, Inayat Khan states, "I was very glad indeed to read your writings. They are the Message, no doubt."[45]

Nargis' own compositions include *Between the Desert and the Sown: The Way of the Disciple* [1923]; *At the Gate of Discipleship* [1924?], *The Lifted Veil*, [1925]; *Wine from the Tavern* [1930?]; the pamphlet *Thoughts are Things: A Gateway to Peace* [1950], and *The Way of Return: A Collection of Mystical Thoughts and Essays*, [1952]. The Sufi Book Depot issued several very brief, undated pamphlets, including the

---

Khan (London: East-West Publications, 1979). 141.

43 Ibid.

44 van Beek, Wil, *Hazrat Inayat Khan: Master of Life, Modern Sufi Mystic* (New York: Vantage Press, 1983), 126.

45 Inayat Khan, letters to Miss Dowland, 1922 {Wissous].

poem "The Song of Return" (also to be found in *The Way of Return*), "In a Rose Garden" (also appearing in *Sufism*, May 1921), and "God the Actor on the Stage of Life" (reprinted from *The Sufi Quarterly* and appearing in *Wine from the Tavern*). Her writings, and particularly her "Teachings Received in the Silence," appear in several Sufi journals and have been reprinted frequently; for example, some of her aphorisms are reproduced in a anonymous publication entitled *The Grape! Vintage from the Sufi Vineyard* (England: Sufi Movement, 19—). This gives some indication of their enthusiastic reception by mureeds and other readers with spiritual interests.

Perhaps Nargis is best known for her *uwaisi* transmissions from Inayat Khan, which she described as "Murshid's inner Teaching as received in the silence and rendered by Nargis." Some of these sayings appear in *Sufism* and in *The Sufi Quarterly*, others in books published by Nargis, and some remain in unpublished manuscripts. These teachings, while they are deeply personal contemplations of the path of discipleship and initiation, at the same time have a universal and timeless quality.

Khalifa Nargis had a highly refined understanding of the initiatic link between murshid and mureed. Her books are, first and foremost, a deeply mystical reflection upon the nature of the spiritual path, an extended contemplation of the meaning of discipleship. At the same time, her approach to spirituality in life was quite practical and grounded. She did not approve of spiritual elitism, posturing, or the sense of being one of the elect. In the passage "Meditation," found in her book *The Way of Return*, Nargis notes:

> *All meditation, occult practice, or striving for self development are quite useless to help a man upon the Spiritual Path in his search for God unless he can bring down to physical plane activities the teaching he receives in this way upon the inner planes, and can live it simply and unobtrusively in his*

> *ordinary daily life. That is the way—the only way—which is allowable or desirable, for any man upon the Path of Return to bring to those with in his circle of influence a knowledge of the Light which is within him.*[46]

Just as her teacher Inayat Khan taught that spirituality is natural, Nargis believed that "Whoever has received spiritual initiation will show in his ordinary life the fruit of the spirit . . . because it is as natural to him as it is natural for an apple tree to bear apples. The fruit may feed many people, but the tree remains unconscious and indifferent as to whom it feeds. Its purpose is to produce fruit and in so doing fulfills its life's purpose."[47] For her, everyday life is the arena in which "the Master's work can and must be done." In the Sufi tradition, she maintained "the secret of balance lies in keeping the eyes of the soul fixed upon God, while the feet are firmly planted upon earth."[48]

Nargis was a sensitive and perceptive soul, acutely aware of the sufferings of humanity. The prominence in her writing of the themes of life's tests and trials and the transmutation of suffering hint at the personal pain she confronted and transformed, realizing the inevitability of suffering in this dualistic material world. Her vision of the inner life was firmly grounded in elevating the condition of the man and woman on the street; she knew that realizing their divine nature, accessing the life of the spirit, could free them from the "prison of matter dense."[49]

Nargis lived through two world wars in Southampton, which, due to its docks and strategic value, was bombed repeatedly by the Nazis. She was there during other catastrophes, such as the sinking of the RMS Titanic (1912), which

46 Dowland, Nargis, *The Way of Return: A Collection of Mystical Thoughts and Essays.* (London: John M. Watkins, 1952),102.

47 Ibid. 117.

48 Dowland, Nargis, *The Lifted Veil.* 43.

49 Dowland, Nargis, "A Message," *The Sufi Quarterly*, 4.2 (Oct. 1920), 7–8.

had sailed out of Southampton. Peter Neal, in his *The Story of Southampton*, quotes the *Daily Mirror* "The agonizing scenes at the docks could move the hardest hearts to compassion" and observes that "Around six hundred homes in Southampton were directly affected by the disaster, and over one hundred children at Northam School lost a parent or relative on the ship. The town had not been dealt such a crushing blow since the French raid nearly six hundred years earlier."[50] The Polygon House Hotel was known to be a favorite venue for passengers sailing out of Southampton on these great ships, so some Titanic passengers would have roomed in the Polygon prior to this tragic voyage.

In her poem "A Message," Nargis wonders how long will "our cities echo shouts of vice, of curses and ribald song," noting how "brute need and its cravings glamours the waking sense":

> *The drunkard with brain besotted, who cares not for Devil or man,*
> *The human vulture preying, the criminal under a ban;*
> *The wanton luxuriously living a life of evil fame,*
> *The woman whose skirts she may not brush*
> *And the man who caused her shame.*[51]

Countering this graphic portrait of human misery, Nargis earmarks within each soul a divine spark, a pristine purity that can never be tarnished. One is reminded of William Blake's *Songs of Experience*; like him, Nargis perceives the "Human Form Divine," however veiled. Had her own master not expressed this thought in his *Gayan* and repeated it with slight variations throughout his work: "Divinity is human perfection and humanity is divine limitation"? Nargis states:

> *All human lives are knit to God through each earth-life to the grave.*

50 Neal, Peter, *The Story of Southampton* (Gloucestershire: The History Press, 2014), 148,

51 Dowland, Nargis, "A Message," The Sufi Quarterly, 4.2 (Oct. 1920), 7–8.

Their souls can never be damned, nor to Hell by a Devil be driven,
'For their angels do always behold the Face of my Father which is in Heaven'
These Angels, in the silence, are teaching each man's soul.[52]

Transcribed in her notebook in the same period, Nargis recounts a rather extraordinary dream in which she sees her murshid "sitting on one of the bridges across the Thames on a bench, with at every side a woman of the street, tired and asleep, resting against him." In asking Murshid (whether literally or "in the silence") about this, she receives a prophecy of a New Age when there will be a "few sowers for the field of God, who may be trusted to sow the living seed, the fruit of which shall be for the healing of nations, the bread of life given without money and without price to all who ask. And in those days, there shall be no starving bodies for they are the result of starving souls."[53]

Nargis was powerfully drawn to the path of comforter and healer. As it was her deep conviction that the Beloved was to be found "on the path which lies between the field of joy and the field of sorrow,"[54] she had found the way to transmute her personal sufferings into joy, as she calls it, "the secret of Divine Alchemy." In *The Lifted Veil*, she writes:

Before the human heart can be tuned to vibrate to the Christ-note, the highest rate of vibration possible to mankind, it must be made capable of response to every note of sorrow and pain, every failure and shortcoming to which man is prone; for he cannot know the highest unless he also knows the lowest, cannot experience Heaven without experience of Hell, cannot know the whole until he knows every part . . . The price of such realization is great indeed, but the reward is far greater, for upon one who has reached this

52 Ibid.

53 Dowland, Nargis, *Miss Dowland's Notebook*.

54 Dowland, Nargis, *Between the Desert and the Sown: The Way of the Disciple* ([Southampton: Sufi Movement, [1923]), 7.

> *stage on the spiritual Path is conferred a title of the highest honour possible of attainment by man, that of THE CONSOLER."*[55]

She recognizes the positive function of pain and sorrow as the "birth-throes of the spirit, and absolutely necessary for its growth.[56]

Nargis' regarded the spiritual path as one simultaneously requiring delicacy and fortitude, unshakable faith, and ultimately surrender. She described it as a journey characterized by "bewilderment, from beginning to end" and used the metaphor of the whirlwind to describe a kind of ravishment of the earnest seeker's soul:

> *. . . Spiritual sight cannot be hastened but must be a gradual unfoldment, and cannot be fully awakened until the mureed is ready to follow the path of the whirlwind.*
>
> *When the whirlwind comes, everything in its path is caught up from earth and whirled round and round in its mighty force, which is never for one second's time stationery, but as it passes, only those atoms which are as light as thistledown and strong as the wind, can follow; the others sink exhausted to earth again.*
>
> *Many are caught, but few can follow.*[57]

Having lived through both World War I, the "Great War," and World War II, Nargis had witnessed the unleashing of previously unimagined powers of destruction, so it is not surprising that one of her great concerns was for world peace and the dawn of a New Age of harmony and understanding among nations. According to Peter Neal, during World War II, "Southampton had been attacked on almost sixty occasions, making it the seventh most bombed town or city in the

55 Dowland, Nargis, *The Lifted Veil* ([Southampton]: Sufi Movement, 1925), 116–117.

56 Dowland, Nargis, *Thoughts Are Things: A Gateway to Peace* (Southampton: Wisemans, [1950?]), 24.

57 Dowland, Nargis, *Between the Desert and the Sown*, 50–51.

country," with "over 30,000 incendiaries . . . as well as over 2500 bombs and many more" with 631 people [who] lost their lives in the attacks and 1,800 . . . injured, half of them seriously."[58] The Polygon had its own special wartime roles to play, having been in the First World War "the headquarters of the British Expeditionary Force, camped out in the hotel; while during the Second World War, the Polygon was headquarters for the 14th Major Port US Army in the lead-up to the D-Day invasion in 1944."[59]

The Sufi Book Depot was located at 54 Above Bar Street. Neal reports that during the Blitz in 1940, Southampton's "central spine of the High Street and Above Bar Street 'had largely crumbled into unrecognisable wreckage.'"[60] In a letter to fellow mureed Angela Alt, Nargis herself alludes to the wartime devastation of her city, "The Wisemans' shop has been demolished entirely, in fact the whole town has almost. They are trying to get a place in Portswood near here. There was no fire fortunately, so they have salvaged a good deal, although everything is covered with dust and dirt. The odd thing is that the very first things which were found are my books and later some of Murshid's, and all these are only dusty; I have them all here now. . . ."[61]

Nargis believed that she was living at the dawn of a New Age "of Life and Light for all men," connecting it with her theme of breaking of forms so that a new dispensation might emerge; she said "it is a red dawn, for before the beginning of any age there is always a time of great desolation, bloodshed and the breaking of every kind of form. This is inevitable."[62]

58 Neal, Peter, *The Story of Southampton*, 192.

59 Hamilton, Keith,"Polygon Ten Years but Not Forgotten." (*Southern Daily Echo*, Apr. 18, 2007).

60 Neal, Peter, *The Story of Southampton*, 183.

61 "Biographical Sketch of Miss Jessie Eliza Dowland (Khalifa Nargis)." *Biography of Pir-o-Murshid Inayat Khan*, 496–97.

62 Dowland, Nargis, *The Way of Return*, 119–120.

In a pamphlet entitled *Thoughts Are Things: A Gateway to Peace*, published in 1950 shortly before her death, Nargis emphasizes that one's thoughts have "form and life, and also a purpose,"[63] so that if one desires to bring about a peaceful world one must focus one's thoughts on peace. Her conviction was that the "model of the plans for world government in the New Age had long been on the mental plane" and this mental vision of "unity and brotherhood for all mankind," if held widely, would eventually manifest on the physical plane.[64]

The advice she shares about the power of entertaining luminous thoughts, as Pir Vilayat Inayat Khan stated it years later in his seminars and lectures, could most certainly have been influenced by Prentice Mulford's book of the same title, *Thoughts Are Things* (1889), and by theosophical works such as *Thought Forms* (1901) by Annie Besant, with whom Nargis' friend and fellow mureed Murshida Saintsbury-Green studied closely before coming to Sufism. In one of her inner teachings received in the silence, Nargis states:

> *Our thoughts, and only our thoughts, make our real environment. If we are continually thinking about God, we are drawn to those great souls who have sought Him in all ages and become one with that wonderful fellowship of illuminated ones . . . We are all seeking the God we have created. At the end of our search we shall find, not God, but ourselves.*[65]

In another letter to Angela Alt that was both enigmatic and prophetic, she stated, " I am sure the seeds he [Inayat Khan] broadcasted are taking root. Everywhere I can see it . . . Much more will be seen after the war has ended and the beginning of the New Age starts . . . The real Message Murshid brought

63 Dowland, Nargis, *Thoughts Are Things*. 3.

64 Dowland, Nargis, *The Way of Return*, 118–119.

65 Dowland, Nargis, unpublished "Inner Teaching As Received in the Silence," 21.0413.

will be given in quite a different form from the Sufi Order as we know it, of that I feel sure."[66]

We do not know Nargis' reaction to Inayat Khan's return to India. In a letter from Delhi dated November 16, 1927, most likely addressed to Murshida Green, Inayat Khan reports that the Sufis "found me out and now I am in the papers," and that he is "invited from universities to lecture"; he continues wearily, "I cannot hide and be alone and quiet, even if I were in a cave of the Himalayas."[67]

One imagines Nargis' heartache if her friend shared this note with her, she who had worked ceaseless to relieve her murshid's burdens, to provide him with homely comforts, unreserved support and, at least on several occasions, a place in the New Forest for the spiritual retreats that were his soul's longing. Her response to the news of Inayat Khan's death in India on February 5, 1927 is not recorded.

Jessie Nargis Dowland resided in Southampton until her death. In the "Biographical Sketches," we are told that Nargis, ever-faithful in her service to the Message, "continued to gather around her the mureeds until her passing away."[68] According to her death certificate, she died of acute bronchitis at the age of eighty-seven, in Southampton on December 29, 1953.[69]

66 "Biographical Sketch of Miss Jessie Eliza Dowland (Khalifa Nargis)," *Biography of Pir-o-Murshid Inayat Khan*, 497.

67 Unpublished letter of Hazrat Inayat Khan to Murshid Sophia Saintsbury-Green (?), (Delhi: Nov. 16, 1926).

68 "Biographical Sketch of Miss Jessie Eliza Dowland (Khalifa Nargis)," *Biography of Pir-o-Murshid Inayat Khan*. 497.

69 "Certified Copy of an Entry of Death." (Southampton: Dec. 31,1953, no. 386).

Index

A

C

D

E

F

(cont. overleaf)

G

H

I

M

N

Q

R

T

Y

For more information on Sufism
and Hazrat Inayat Khan please visit
www.inayatiorder.org